healthy greek food

traditional fish taverna on Hydra island

tables next to the Aegean Sea

Alekos Valavanis

healthy greek food

ingredients and recipes of the mediterranean diet

TRANSLATION
Sunny A. Angeles

contributors

MANAGING EDITOR
Alekos Valavanis

PHOTOGRAPHERS
Yiannis Vaharidis: *page 2-3,12,22,32,33,98,103,*
104,106,110,112,114,116,121,122,123,125,126,129,131,132,
146,148,151,153,155,159,161,164,167,171,179,181,182,183,
185,189,191,193,195,199,201,202,205,206,209,213,214

Yiorgos Depollas: *page 6-7,8,11,16,19,20,21,22,44,*
45,47,48,49,50,51,52,53,55,57,58,59,62,63,66,67,69,
72,73,78,82,97,111,113,118,163,172,176,186,196,197,218

Dimitris Pazaitis: *page 11,15,16,18,34,65,81,83,*
85,89,91,93,95,137,139,156,211,217

Alekos Valavanis: *page 5,11,14,16,18,23,24,26,27,*
29,30,38,39,40,42,46,54,56,60,61,64,68,70,71,74,75,
76,77,87,92,108,109,134,140,142,169,175

TRANSLATOR
Sunny A. Angeles

HOME ECONOMIST and FOOD STYLIST
Daphne Muha

ART DIRECTOR
Stavrielena Dimitrakopoulou

IMAGE PROCESSING
Yiota Makropoulou

COLOR SEPARATIONS
Toxo Co.

Published in Greece by
EDITIONS FOTORAMA Co.
52 Sina Street, Athens, GR-10672
Telephone: + 30 210 3643 592
Fax: + 30 210 3643 323
http://www.fotorama.gr
e-mail: info@fotorama.gr

ISBN: 960-7524-15-2

The chapter on wild edible greens could not have been written without the in-depth knowledge
*of my friend and best man **Kosta Kazamiaki,** an authority on the wild edible flora of our country.*
I owe him heartfelt thanks for enabling me to discover their fascinating varities.

I thank my mother Vasso for her valuable help with the chapter on pies,
which reflects her skill with the traditional recipes of Epirus.

I warmly thank the translator of the English edition, Sunny A. Angeles, for her valuable help.
Apart from translating, she also helped significantly in all the chapters, particularly the section on olive oil,
which displays her special knowledge of its properties and uses.

pumpkin

almond blossoms

variety of dried beans

sun-dried tomatoes

contents

raw spiny chicory (stamnagáthi)
with olive oil and lemon juice

author's
prologue

While travelling through Greece one discovers that it is a country worth visiting not only for its sights but also for its tastes. The rhythms of nature are expressed in the daily lives of the people. Their dietary customs reflect the landscape and satisfy the senses.

We are a part of our environment and are defined by what we partake of it. We emit and receive feelings and thoughts which shape us. And the foods we choose determine our physical and spiritual health. We live in a society where there is an over-abundance of material goods, yet few foods can be considered absolutely pure.

The sins of the contemporary diet are many: over-consumption of fats, sugar and meat, chemical pesticides that have poisoned our grains, fruit and

Alekos Valavanis was born in Athens in 1955 to a family with roots in Epirus. He is a photographer and co-founder of Editions Fotorama. Alongside his professional work, he has made a systematic study of traditional Greek foods for the last several years, discovering and documenting the varieties of produce, wine, olives and olive oil cultivation.

His first book, *Original Greek Cooking*, a collection of native recipes, was published in 1993 and has been translated into nine languages.

vegetables, and genetically modified organisms. The only way to ensure nutritional balance is to carefully select the foods we eat.

This compact book presents the basic ingredients of the healthy Greek diet, the quintessence of the famous Mediterranean diet, together with recipes from the inexhaustible Greek tradition.

Alekos Valavanis

mediterranean diet

Mesoyiakí dhiatrofí

THE FRUGAL DIET OF THE GREEKS

As international interest grows in the nutritional habits of the peoples of the world, the benefits of the Greek diet are increasingly evident. Throughout the ages Greek cuisine has maintained its frugality, relying mainly on local produce rather than imports. Archaeological findings and historical texts substantiate that the Greek diet has always been simple.

Pericles mentions the refined abstemiousness of the Athenians of the classical period, who although able to choose a large variety of foods from the entire known world, were known for "attic dining", which means a spare table.

Ancient Sparta was so renowned for discipline that its name is an English by-word for austerity. The Spartans were just as discliplined in their diet, characterised by a plain black broth called *mélana zomó*. The modern Mediterranean diet is based on the dietary habits prevalent in Greece, and particularly Crete, as they evolved through the centuries.

What are the staples of the Mediterranean diet and why is it considered ideal? In the 60s the World Health Organisation conducted research in seven countries (Finland, the US, the Netherlands, Italy, Yugoslavia, Japan and Greece) to determine which populations had the smallest percentage of deaths from cancer and cardiovascular disease. After ten

years this study came to an incredible conclusion.

The people who live in Greece, especially on Crete, enjoy one of the longest average lifespans in the world. The researchers discovered that for 35 centuries, since the Minoan civilisation, Greeks have been eating almost the same foods.

Their everyday diet consisted of abundant cereals (bread and rusks). They regularly ate pulses [legumes] such as chick peas, broad beans, beans and lentils. They gathered a wide variety of wild greens and herbs, and cultivated vegetables.

The only cooking fat was extra virgin olive oil, and they ate a lot of olives. They also ate a lot of fish and seafood. They gathered nuts such as almonds, walnuts, pistachios and chestnuts, which they ate unprocessed, and fresh fruit including figs, pears, apples and pomegranates.

Their flocks of sheep and goats gave them milk from which they made yoghurt and cheese; they rarely slaughtered the animals to eat their flesh. They kept many bee hives to supply them with good, pure honey. They made their own wine which they always drank in moderation.

It is easy to see that not a single essential nutrient is missing from this dietary model.

Unrefined cereals and pulses [legumes] provide abundant complex carbohydrates for energy and almost the entire Vitamin B complex to enable the nervous system to function well.

Fresh fruits and vegetables supply essential Vitamins A and C to give the organism a defence against infection.

Cholesterol-free olive oil helps blood circulation and is rich in Vitamin E to keep cells young.

Milk, yoghurt and cheese contain calcium which is essential for strong bones and teeth.

Fresh fish and seafood supply proteins necessary for growth and essential fatty acids for good heart function.

Nuts, greens, pulses [legumes] and honey add essential amino acids, minerals and trace elements.

The Mediterranean Diet Pyramid

At the base of the Mediterranean diet are the complex carbo-hydrates (cereals, bread and pasta), which together with fresh fruits, vegetables and greens constitute 60% of the diet.

Pulses [legumes] and nuts add another 15%; olive oil, olives and dairy products 7%. Fish and seafood add 5%, poultry and eggs 3%. Finally, sweets, meat and red wine contribute a mere 1% each.

olive oil
and olives

Eleólado ke eliés

olive tree on the archaeological site of Mycenae

History

The olive tree first appeared in the Mediterranean before the dawn of history. It is intimately connected with the lives, the myths and the history of the peoples who live in this area.

The olive tree first began to be cultivated about 7,000 years ago. The wild olive tree from which the cultivated species originated probably came to Greece from Asia Minor. On Crete, cultivation of the olive must have begun around 3500 B.C. and contributed significantly to the growth of the Minoan civilisation. To the ancient Greeks the olive symbolised prosperity, peace, fertility and fruitfulness. It was indisputably a particularly valuable tree for humans. According to mythology the olive was the gift of the goddess Athena to the inhabitants of the city of Athens, who as a sign of their gratitude gave the name of the goddess to their city.

The Ancient Greeks anointed their bodies and hair with olive oil for beauty and for health. The prize for the winners of the ancient Olympic Games was a wreath of olive leaves. Hippocrates (c.460 - c.370 B.C.), the father of modern medicine, called olive oil a "great healer". Homer compared it to "liquid gold". Innumerable Greek and Roman writings mention the olive and its benefits. References to the olive can be found in both the Bible and the Koran.

The Ancient Greeks took the olive tree with them to their colonies in Magna Graecia (Italy). The Romans in turn spread the olive throughout their vast empire. After the 16th century the Europeans brought the olive to the New World, and it began to be cultivated in California, Mexico, Peru, Chile and Argentina. More recently cultivation has also begun in Australia and South Africa. It is estimated that today there are more than 750,000,000 olive trees in the world, of which the over-

whelming majority, about 715,000,000, are in Mediterranean countries. Throughout the millennia of its history the olive tree has grown in perfect harmony with nature and the civilisations in the countries around the Mediterranean basin, particularly in Greece, where conditions remain ideal for it to flourish at its best.

The tree

The olive tree (Olea europaea L OLEACEAE) is an evergreen with long narrow leaves that are dark green on one side and silvery on the other. The tree varies in height from three to 12 metres. The tree ages very well, and its natural lifespan is 300 to 600 years, though there are trees that are believed to be over 1,000 years old. It grows in temperate and sub-tropical climates, and cannot survive sub-zero temperatures. It can withstand droughts and strong winds. The tree does not bear fruit for the first three or four years of its life, and does not attain full development until it is twenty years old. It blossoms in spring and is fertilised by the wind. The fruit ripens six to eight months after the tree blossoms. The unripe green olives turn purple and eventually black when they ripen, and cling to the branches for several weeks after that. Table olives can be harvested either green or black, while for olive oil the olives must not be green.

The olive and literature

The olive tree and its fruit have inspired many writers throughout the world.

Thomas Jefferson: "The olive tree is surely the richest gift from Heaven."

Aldous Huxley: "...I like them all, but especially the olive. For what it symbolises, first of all, peace with its leaves and joy with its golden oil."

Federico Garcia Lorca: "Angels with long braids and hearts of olive oil."

Lawrence Durrell (*Prospero's Cell*): "The entire Mediterranean seems to rise out of the sour pungent taste of black olives

olive tree on the
archaeological site of Delphi

between the teeth. A taste older than meat or wine, a taste as old as cold water. Only the sea itself seems as ancient a part of the region as the olive and its oil, that like no other products of nature, have shaped civilizations from remotest antiquity to the present."

Extra virgin olive oil

How extra virgin olive oil is produced

The way extra virgin olive oil is produced has remained essentially the same over the millennia despite developments in technology which have made the task easier.

1 The fruit is gathered from November to March

For the best quality of olive oil the fruit must be harvested when its colour begins to change from green to purplish-black. This is when the oil content of the fruit increases and the flavour is at its best. The fruit must be picked the traditional way: by hand. The labourers spread nets under the trees to catch the olives, then rake the branches or beat them with rods, taking care not to bruise the fruit. The olives are then put into fabric sacks and taken to the oil mills as quickly as possible, within the same or at the very latest the following day. This is because if the olives are left any longer they begin to ferment, spoiling the flavour of the oil. In regions where the olives are permitted to ripen and fall off the trees by themselves (for instance, on Corfu) the oil is of poor quality.

2 Processing the fruit

To obtain the oil, the olive fruit is crushed mechanically. Nowadays the olives, after first being washed to remove dirt and leaves, are crushed by machines with a stainless steel pulper, followed by a process to press the pulp to extract the oil. The process must not exceed 25 °C. The olive pulp is then kneaded with water. The ensuing juice is centrifuged to separate the oil from the water. Finally, the oil is filtered to remove any sediment. In the old days people used large round millstones to crush the fruit and extract the oil, a practice that is returning to favor. Extra virgin olive oil is the only kind of oil which is edible just the way it comes from the fruit.

cold pressing of olive pulp in a traditional olive mill

Oil-producing varieties

There are many varieties of olives, but some are better suited for producing olive oil because of their greater oil content. The main oil producing varieties, with their local names:

Olea europea var. argentata L OLEACEAE, *(Megharítiki, Hondroliá, Perachorítiki)* is cultivated mainly in Attica and Boeotia. It contains 29% oil which is usually of good quality.

Olea europea var. craneomorpha L OLEACEAE, *(Lianoliá Kérkiras, Dafnófilli, Striftoliá, Neroliá, Suvloli, Prevezána, Korfoliá, Korfiátiki)* is cultivated on the Ionian Islands and the coastal regions of Epirus. It contains 20% oil which is of very good quality as long as harvest is not delayed (which unfortunately is not usually the case).

Olea europea var. mamilaris L OLEACEAE, *(Tsunáti, Mastoidhés, Mastoliá, Muratoliá)* is cultivated mainly in Rethymnon, Chania, Laconia and Messinia. It contains 25% oil of very good quality.

Olea europea var. mastoides L OLEACEAE, *(Koronéiki, Ladholiá, Psiloliá, Mikrókarpi, Lianoliá)* is perhaps the most important variety in Greece. Cultivated on Crete, the Peloponnese, the Ionian Islands, the eastern Aegean and elsewhere, it has a small fruit that contains up to 24% oil of exceptional taste and aroma.

Olea europea var. media subrotunda L OLEACEAE, *(Adhramitiní, Mitiliniá, Aivaliótiki)* originated in Asia Minor and is cultivated mainly on Lesbos, Chios and Euboia. It contains 22-25% thin oil of exceptional quality with a distinctive taste.

Olea europea var. microcarpa subrotunda L OLEACEAE, *(Mirtoliá, Smertoliá, Murtoliá)* is cultivated mainly in Laconia. A small fruit that contains up to 24% oil of good quality.

Olea europea var. microphylla L OLEACEAE, *(Kutsureliá, Ladholiá, Patriní, Kurteliá)* is cultivated mainly in Aeghialia, Corinth and Aetoloakarnania. It contains 24% oil of average quality.

Olea europea var. ovalis L OLEACEAE, *(Aghuromanáki, manáki)* is cultivated mainly in Argholidha, Corinth, Arcadia, Spetses. It contains 25% oil of good quality.

Olea europea var. pyiriformis L OLEACEAE, *(Valanoliá, Valána)* is one of the best oil-producing varieties, and is cultivated mainly on Lesbos, Chios and Skyros. It contains 25-30% oil of exceptional quality.

Types of olive oil

The term "virgin" means that the oil is extracted from the fruit naturally, only by mechanical means (pressure or centrifuge) after the washed olives are crushed and kneaded with water. Virgin olive oils suitable for human consumption which may be labelled "natural" are divided into various grades:

Extra virgin olive oil: the best quality of olive oil. It must not contain more than 0.8% acidity (0.8g of oleic acid per 100g of oil). The better quality oils have even less (below 0.5% acidity), a grade sometimes known as extrissima. This grade has exceptional organoleptic characteristics (aroma, taste and colour).

Virgin olive oil—fine: a virgin olive oil with organoleptic characteristics similar to those of extra virgin, but with up to 1.5% acidity.

Virgin olive oil—semi-fine or curante: a virgin olive oil with good taste and aroma, and acidity up to 3.3%.

The other grades of olive oil are not fit for human consumption without first being chemically refined.

Virgin olive oil—lampante: although this is also a virgin oil, it has a bad taste and smell, or its acidity is over 3.3%. It needs to be refined, or is used in industries such as soap production.

Refined olive oil: This is obtained from lampante virgin olive oil by refining with chemical bleaches and deodorisers, which however do not alter the original structure of the glycerides. It is odourless, tasteless, and cannot be consumed as is.

Olive oil (formerly also known as "pure" olive oil): This is refined olive oil to which some virgin olive oil is added in varying proportions to render it more palatable.

Olive-Pomace oil: This is obtained by chemical solvents from the olive pits and other solids that remain after the virgin oil has been extracted. In Greece this is usually only used to burn in votive candles in front of icons.

Extra virgin olive and health

Hippocrates was the first to recognise the beneficial qualities of extra virgin olive oil. He recommended it to cure ulcers, muscular pains and other illnesses. Many studies have since proven its role in the prevention of various types of cancers. It is also a very important factor in the reduction of cardio-vascular disease, particularly because of its effects on blood cholesterol.

It is probably no coincidence that Cretans enjoy the longest average lifespan in Europe, with the lowest incidence of cardiovascular and related diseases, while Greek women have a significantly lower rate of breast cancer. This is to a great

final stages of cold-pressing extra virgin olive oil in a traditional olive mill

extent due to the copious use of olive oil and the Greek diet in general. (Average consumption of olive oil in Greece is around 20 litres per annum per capita, by far the highest in the world, while on Crete it can reach double that amount.) The traditional Greek cuisine is the epitome of what is known as the Mediterranean diet, which has in recent years been growing in popularity in Europe, America and Asia. The staples of this "diet" are extra virgin olive oil, olives, pulses [legumes], cereals including pasta, lots of fruit and vegetables, some dairy products, fish and poultry, with red meat kept to a minimum. Traditionally, meals are accompanied by a glass of red wine.

The advantages of extra virgin olive oil

1 Extra virgin olive oil is produced by purely mechanical means, without any chemicals being used at any stage as is the case with less than virgin grades of olive oil and all vegetable oils.
2 It is a predominantly monounsaturated fat which reduces the "bad" LDL (low density lipo-protein) cholesterol which clogs arteries, while not reducing the "good" HDL (high density lipoprotein) as polyunsaturated oils do.
3 It contains all the essential fatty acids that cannot be synthesised by the body.
4 It contains natural antioxidants (tocopherols) which prevent the oxidation of fatty acids, thus protecting from arteriosclerosis.
5 It does not cause gallstones, unlike vegetable oils.
6 It passes through the stomach faster than vegetable oils and animal fats, creating less pressure on the lower oesophageal sphincter, and does not cause heartburn and indigestion.

*detail of an olive oil storage jar
of the Minoan period
(archaeological site of Knossos)*

7 It aids the good function of the pancreas.

8 It aids the good function of the colon.

9 It can withstand deep frying at 200°C for two hours without breaking down and releasing toxic substances as vegetable oils do. Unlike the latter it can be reused safely several times.

10 It complements the taste of other foods but, because of its own rich flavour, large quantities are not required

What the experts say

A study from the **University of Oxford**, UK, suggested olive oil may protect against heart disease by aiding the immune system. Researchers compared the effects of a diet high in monounsaturated fat, such as olive oil, to the typical United Kingdom diet, that is higher in polyunsaturated fat, among 60 middle-aged men. Over a two-month period, the diet high in olive oil significantly lowered blood levels of adhesion molecules that result when inflammation of the arteries occurs. Chronic inflammation damages arteries, which can lead to arteriosclerosis. A decrease in adhesion molecules may indicate another means by which olive oil protects against this disease.

The **American Heart Association** found in researching the modern day diet that Greece and especially the island of Crete had the lowest mortality rate due to cardiovascular illness.

Finland and the United States had the highest mortality rate. The only notable difference between the countries was the type of fat ingested.

Jean Carper, a leading authority on health and nutrition, an award-winning correspondent for CNN, author of *The Food Pharmacy* and *Food-Your Miracle Medicine* and a nationally syndicated columnist:

"I love the whole idea of olive oil's versatility. I use it for baking, as well as salad dressings and sautéing. Olive oil has been around for a long time, and the more we know about it, the more we learn about its great contribution to good health."

Dr Demetrius Trichopoulos, chairman of the **Department of Epidemiology, Harvard University School of Public Health**:

"I like the taste of olive oil. And, because olive oil

is so flavourful, a little goes a long way while cooking, which is great for people like me who watch their fat intake."

Bruno Berra, Faculty of Pharmacy, University of Milan:

"An 'American version' of the Mediterranean diet was developed, meeting all the nutritional guidelines of the United States. The feasibility and acceptability of the diet amongst healthy American adults and subjects who had recently survived a myocardial infarction were very good."

Dr Barbara Levine, director of **the Nutrition Information Centre at New York Hospital:**

"Olive oil has a protective effect against some types of malignant tumours: prostate, breast, colon, squamous cell, and oesophageal."

Dr Peck, School of Medicine, University. of Miami:
"In vitro and in vivo (in animals), the minor polar components of extra virgin olive oil increase significantly the resistance of LDL to oxidation."

Composition of olive oil

Olive oil constituents can be divided into two categories: the saponifiable fraction (triacylglycerols, FFA, phospatides) and the unsaponifiable fraction (hydrocarbon, fatty alcohols).

The unsaponifiable constituents of virgin olive oil account for 0.5 to 1.5% of the oil, while in olive pomace oil these constituents are about 2.5%. Some of the non-glycerine constituents (unsaponifiable matter) contribute to the flavour quality of the extra virgin olive oil.

Taste

Just like good wine, every extra virgin olive oil can be judged according to its taste, colour, organoleptic characteristics and acidity. Every extra virgin olive oil is unique since it is the result of particular conditions such as the soil, the climate, the variety and age of the olive trees, the season when the fruit was harvested, and how it was processed.

The colour of Greek extra virgin olive oil is predominantly a golden green, but the variations in shades are many. The taste can be mild or strong, even peppery. When extra virgin olive oil is milled properly it preserves all the aroma, vitamins and taste of the fruit from which it came. To see for yourself the subtle difference between the extra virgin olive oils of different regions or olive varieties, cut some slices of white bread into morsels. Pour a small quantity of each extra virgin olive oil onto separate small white plates. Examine the difference in colour and texture of each oil by swirling it around on the plate to release the aroma, then bring it close to your nose

and take a deep breath to inhale its bouquet. You will see that there are differences from oil to oil. Dip a small piece of bread into the oil and try the taste and texture of the oil, and note the aftertaste that lingers in the mouth.

Useful information

Extra virgin olive oil's enemies are air, heat and light. The best way to store extra virgin olive oil is in airtight containers far from heat and light. In this way it can be stored up to two years.

There is no need for cold storage of extra virgin olive oil. Refrigerated extra virgin olive oil turns cloudy or even solidifies. This does not affect the oil in any way, and if left at room temperature the oil soon returns to its original state. Many people believe that the best extra virgin olive oil is green. However, the colour is not a reliable indicator of quality or taste. Oils of exceptional quality vary both in colour and in taste.

Extra virgin olive oil can be used for all forms of cooking: frying, baking, roasting, boiling or sautéing, and of course raw on salads, cooked vegetables, pulses [legumes], feta cheese, grilled fish, bread, or swirled into soups just before serving. Olive oil has the highest smoking point of any vegetable oil, making it ideal for frying and deep-frying. However, do not let it overheat, and be sure to strain it after each use.

Olive oil contains the same number of calories as any other fat, be it of vegetable or animal origin, 9.3 per gram. Up to 98% of olive oil can be absorbed by the human organism. Due to this it facilitates the absorption of the fat-soluble vitamins it contains. (Only the fat of human breast milk is absorbed at a greater rate.)

olive oil flavoured with
rosemary, bay leaf,
pepper corns and chilli peppers

Table Olives

Olive as food

Table olives are a hallmark of the Greek diet. They are a unique food and have undergone very little change over the millennia of their history. If we try to eat olives straight off the tree we can see that they are bitter. This is because substances in the skin of the olive are bitter.

The most important varieties of table olives:

Olea europea var. ceraticarpa, Kalamátas is the most important table olive, cultivated mainly in Messinia and surrounding regions (in the Peloponnese).

It has the largest leaves of any variety of olives.

Olea europea var. rotunda, Konservoliá, Aghιniníu, Ἀmfissas, **Hondroliá,** has large round fruit with very good flavour, processed when green, black or "blond". It is cultivated in Agrinio, Amphissa and elsewhere.

Olea europea var. media oblonga, Thrúmba, Thasίtiki, **Thrumboliá, Stafidholiá,** is a favourite of Greeks, cultivated on the islands of the Aegean Sea. It wrinkles naturally on the tree because of a fungus, *Phoma deae*, which gives a dis-tinctive taste to the fruit.

Olea europea var. minor rotunda, Manáki, Kothréiki, **Ghlykomanáki,** has medium-sized round fruit with a distinctive sweet taste, processed when black. This olive is also used for olive oil. It is cultivated in the Peloponnese and Euboea, in Attica and elsewhere.

Olea europea var. maxima, Karidholiá,
Stravoliá, is a variety with two distinctive seams. It is cultivated in mainland Greece, Mitilini and elsewhere.

olive oil flavoured with oregano, capers, bay leaf and chilli peppers

kalamáta olives

green olives (prasinoliés)

wrinkled olives (thrúmbes)

Olea europea var. rubrotunda, Prasinoliá, Strongiloliá, Miloliá, is cultivated in Halkidhiki for its large green fruit.

Ways of processing olives

To debitter olives so they become edible requires processing in one of several ways which have remained almost unaltered since antiquity.

To process green olives

1 kg large unripe green olives
1 lt lukewarm water
100g salt
1 lemon, sliced
1 Tbsp oregano or thyme
3-4 Tbsp extra virgin olive oil

Crushed Green Olives

1 Crush olives with a smooth stone or other heavy object (taking care that the pit is not broken) and place them in a container filled with water.

2 Soak them for 8 to 10 days, covering them with a weight to make sure they are all submerged and change the water twice daily until they lose their bitterness (taste to check).

3 Make the brine by stirring the salt into the warm water until it dissolves. Place the olives in a large jar, cover with the brine, add the lemon slices and

oregano or thyme, cover the surface with the extra virgin olive oil and seal the jar.

Crushed olives must be eaten quickly, they do not keep long (no more than 2-4 months) because they change colour and spoil.

To check that the brine is salty enough, carefully add a washed whole egg. If it floats and the part of the shell rising above the surface of the water is the size of a thumbnail it is just right.

You may add flavourings such as pieces of lemon or orange, bay leaf, oregano, thyme or fennel fronds. Seal the jar well.

Green Olives in Brine

1 Place the olives in a large container, cover them with water and make sure they are all submerged. Soak them for about 20 days, changing the water once daily, until they are no longer bitter (taste to check).

2 Make the brine as in the previous recipe (one part of salt in ten parts of warm water). Layer the olives with the lemon slices, cover with the brine, add the extra virgin olive oil and seal the jar.

To process black olives

1 kg large firm ripe black olives ('Amphissa, Kalamáta or any other variety you like)
100g coarse salt (more for salt-cured black olives)

2-4 Tbsp vinegar
3-4 Tbsp extra virgin olive oil

Salt-Cured Black Olives

1 Place olives in a jar, alternating with layers of coarse salt.

2 Leave for 20 days, shaking from time to time. After a few days, when they begin to exude their bitter juices, add a little more salt.

3 When they are no longer bitter (taste to check) add lukewarm water to cover, the vinegar and the olive oil.

4 After a few days they are ready to eat. As the jar gets empty it is good to discard some of the brine so the olives are always barely covered.

Slashed Kalamata Olives in Vinegar

1 With a sharp knife slash each olive lengthwise, taking care the pit is not cut. Soak for 12-15 days, changing the water daily.

2 When they are no longer bitter (taste to check) make the brine as in the first recipe.

3 Place the olives in a jar, add the brine, 3-4 Tbsp vinegar, shake lightly, cover surface with the olive oil and seal the jar.

wild edible greens άγρια χόρτα

ágria hórta

A PILGRIMAGE TO THE EARTH

The goods necessary for our health and wellbeing have been given to us, they are there for the taking all around us, but we find it difficult to recognise them because we have distanced ourselves from nature as never before...

Wild greens and their edible leaves, roots, flowers and seeds were among the first foods of humans since the beginning of their existence. It was only later, in the Neolithic period, that agriculture was organised. In Greece the climate and the abundance of the local flora made the conditions right for humans to establish flourishing permanent settlements. In this blessed land more than 6,000 types of plants have been recorded to date, with new ones continuing to be discovered, making Greece the wealthiest source of plant life in Europe and one of the richest in the world. This truly unique and impressive flora results from geographic location, geological formations, rivers, mountains, ravines, islands and lakes, which combine to create a climate which is particularly favourable for the growth of plant colonies.

Wild edible greens are a significant component of what is called the **'healthy Greek diet'**. Vegetarianism has deep and strong roots in this country, from antiquity to today. Greeks eat large quantities of greens and vegetables, and thay are a basic ingredient in many local dishes. The 'oily dishes' (ladherá), vegetables cooked in extra virgin olive oil, are a

staple of the Greek diet. Raw wild greens are also used skilfully to add flavour to salads.

In many of the colder mountainous regions of Greece (Epirus, Roumeli, Macedonia) olive oil was hard to come by, so cooks instead used milk, feta cheese and butter in many dishes, particularly in pies. In the Ionian Islands a popular dish is *tsigharéli,* a mixture of sweet and bitter greens, sautéed with oil and onion.

In Crete, the Peloponnese and all other regions with a large production of olive oil, 'oily dishes' with greens predominate in the local cuisine, and always include some of the fragrant greens such as Hartwort (*Tordylium apulum,* Fennel (*Foeniculum vulgare*).

Wild greens appear with the first rains in autumn, and are available until the end of spring. They are a traditional alternative in the winter months when not many garden vegetables are available. In summer there are fewer greens, and those that do grow are weeds that spring up among the cultivated vegetables, such as Amaranth (*Amaranthus hybridus*), Mustard (*Sinapis alba*) and Purslane (*Portulaca oleracea*).

The humble wild greens are an excellent source of fibre, vitamins and minerals. What is perhaps less well known is

salsify blossom (lagóhorto) in its immature (left) and seed-bearing (right) stages

their high flavonoid content, which is associated with protection against heart disease and cancer.

Another very important factor which contributes to their superiority in taste is the fact that wild greens are not watered. Studies in the last century have shown that plants develop a defence system when they live in a dry, inhospitable environment, with 'weapons' ranging from thorns, needles and toughness to a strong smell by producing resin. That is what makes them far tastier than cultivated, protected and sheltered greens.

This book introduces the most important edible greens that grow wild in the Greek countryside. I hope that the reader will be encouraged to discover this wondrous world full of hidden treasures, and sample this fundamental and valuable staple of the healthy Greek diet.

GATHERING WILD GREENS AND HERBS

Be careful when gathering wild greens. Eat only the ones you know or recognise. If you are unsure about any, try the sniff test: nearly all poisonous greens have a heavy unpleasant smell that will put you off.

Common names vary from region to region, so the only certain way of recognising them is from their photographs

mallow (molóha)
with blossoms

and their scientific Latin names. (Translator's note: Only a few of these local names have been given, with the most common one first, to enable readers who live in Greece, or tourists visiting Greece, to identify these greens when they go shopping or order them in a restaurant. Please see page 219 for a key to the transliteration).

With most greens the edible portion is the leaves and a part of the root, with a few only the root is edible. In most cases it is good to gather the plant in such a way that a portion of the roots remains in the ground, so that it will spring up again. In this way we can continue harvesting the plant, particularly the rare types, and ensure that the balance of nature is not adversely affected.

Avoid gathering greens in regions that are not clean, such as footpaths, busy roads and areas frequented by animals.

Never gather greens from fields that are sprayed with pesticides and other toxic chemicals, especially in spring.

Do not uproot any greens that you do not intend to consume, nor gather more than you can eat.

Herbs should be gathered in the afternoon so they contain more essential oils.

Do not leave the greens sitting around in plastic bags, especially in the sun, as they quickly wilt.

CLEANING AND PRESERVING WILD GREENS AND HERBS

Cut away any dry parts of the greens and slash a cross in the root section, if thick, so it cooks more quickly.

Wash very thoroughly in plenty of water to get rid of earth and grit. Wilted greens can be refreshed by soaking in cold water for a little while.

Most wild greens can be stored in the refrigerator, unwashed, for 4-6 days. They can be frozen for 6-8 months after blanching in boiling water for 5'.

Herbs are tied in small bunches and hung upside down to dry in a shady, ventilated area. They will keep for quite a few months in airtight jars.

HOW TO EAT WILD GREENS

The best way is to eat wild greens raw, which as with all fresh produce, preserves all their precious nutrients and taste unaltered. Greens that are to be eaten raw must be dried very thoroughly after washing, using a salad spinner or leaving to drain in a colander. Then add extra virgin olive oil and lemon juice or vinegar, tossing well to coat all over.

A combination of different greens, bitter, sweet, fragrant, spicy in taste, turns salads into a real gourmet experience.
Cooked greens are usually simply boiled. It is important to know the taste of each green (bitter or sweet) in order to combine them in a way that balances each dish.

To boil greens

- Bring a little water to a rolling boil in a large saucepan, then add the greens (bitter greens need more water than sweet ones).
- Boil over a high heat with a lid on the saucepan for about 10'-15', testing the greens from time to time to check when done.
- Just before the end of the cooking time add salt (1 tsp per 3 lt of water). Remove the greens from the pot by using two forks, tongs or a slotted spoon so any grit stays on the bottom of the saucepan.

- Add extra virgin olive oil and lemon juice and toss well. The cooking liquor that remains in the pot after boiling many kinds of greens, such as Wild Chicory (*Cichorium intibus*), Sowthistle (*Sonchus oleraceus*) and Asparagus (*Asparagus acutifolius*), makes a tasty drink that is good for you. Simply strain and add a little lemon juice and extra virgin olive oil.

MEDICINAL USES

For many centuries physicians used wild greens and herbs for treating illnesses. Herbalists of the 19th and 20th centuries always extolled the pharmaceutical qualities of the plants native to Greece. When medicine became an established science people stopped going to these herbal practitioners for treatment. Yet these folk remedies were often the basis for the creation of modern medicines.

The pharmaceutical qualities of greens and herbs are provided for information only. No self-treatment should be based on this information without a doctor's approval.

spiny chicory (stamnagáthi) on a beach of Attica

chicory
wild succory

Cichorium intybus

Radhíkia, radhíki ághrio (wild chicory), radhíki tu vunù (mountain chicory), pikralídha (something bitter), kihóri, pikromárulo (bitter lettuce), pikrorádhiko (bitter chicory) kreatorádhiko, stravóxilo.

The most important category of greens in Greece is the Chicory family, which has many varieties, with names that vary considerably from region to region. Nearly all are perennials with a milky juice. From the first rains in autumn until the end of spring the countryside fills with many different kinds of Wild Chicories.

Not to be confused with the cultivated salad leaves which are called chicory or Belgian endive.

History Theophrastus calls it *kichórion*, and Dioscorides *pikrís ágria* (wild bitter). Until a few decades ago a coffee substitute was made from its root.

Properties The chicories contain the tonic bitter substances lactucine and lactupicrine.

A traditional though not always accurate way of easily distinguishing sweet from bitter is their colour: bitter ones have white stems while sweet ones have red.

Uses In salads, on their own or combined with other greens. They go particularly well with sweet greens such as Sowthistles. The cooking liquor is excellent, drunk hot with salt, extra virgin olive oil and lemon juice.

Folk medicine All the Wild Chicories are believed to stimulate the appetite, aid digestion and be good for the stomach. They are diuretic.

spiny chicory
sea chicory

Cichorium spinosum

Stamnagáthi, radhíki tis thálasas (sea chicory)

A favourite green on Crete which has become rare in recent years because it is gathered so intensively. Grows mainly near the sea, in southern Greece, the Aegean islands and Crete. Characterised by the spiny bush that surrounds it. Can be eaten raw or boiled.

dandelion

Taraxacum officinale

Taráxaco, aghrioradhíki (wild chicory),
pikralídha (something bitter),
pikromárulo (bitter lettuce)

A perennial within the same family as Chicory,
with important pharmaceutical qualities.

History The name of the genus
Taraxacum is derived from the
Ancient Greek word *tarássein*,
which means to disturb,
referring to the diuretic properties of
the plant, which would cause increased
micturition and 'disturb' the sleep of those who
had eaten it the previous evening.
It is mentioned by Theophrastus. Its English
name is derived from the French *dent-de-lion*
which ultimately traces back to the Ancient
Greek *odóntos* (tooth) and *léon* (lion), after
the jagged shape of the leaves.

Properties Intensely bitter taste.

Uses Mainly boiled, on its own or combined with
others to tone down its bitterness.

Folk medicine One of the most useful natural
remedies. Diuretic, tonic, stomachic, cholagogue.
Promotes appetite, purifies the blood, counteracts
diabetes. Helps improve the function of the liver
and the gall bladder and is an excellent tonic for
atonic dyspepsia.

dandelion (pikralídha)

stravóxilo,
the most bitter chicory

meat-chicory (kreatorádhiko)

bitter chicory (pikralídha)

wild chicory (radhíki ághrio)

hiromurídas shoots

chicory shoots

provátza

purslane
wild purslane, yellow portulaca

Portulaca oleracea

Chlistrídha, adhráhli, andrákla

Has recently become more widely known in America and Europe after studies showing that thanks to its high linoleic acid content it helps to clear fatty deposits blocking arteries, and fights high serum cholesterol. Annual self-propagating weed springing up among cultivated crops in many parts of Greece. Can even be grown easily in pots.

History Dioscorides, Theophrastus and Galen refer to it as *andráchne* and record its significant pharmaceutical qualities in detail.

Properties Fleshy leaves and stems with a cool, slightly salty taste.

Uses Added raw to summer salads, which it complements with its refreshing taste. Can also be boiled as a salad, accompanied by garlic sauce (skordhaliá, see recipe on page 127).

Folk medicine Diuretic, choleretic. Good against scurvy due to its high Vitamin C content. The linolenic acid it contains fights heart disease and serum cholesterol.

mustard
field mustard, charlock

Sinapis alba, S. nigra, S. arvensis, S. incana
Vrúva, lefkó sinapi (white mustard),
lapsána, lapsanóvruva

One of the 'trinity', along with
the Chicories and Sowthistle,
of the most well-known greens
in Greece. The common name
in modern Greek, *vrúves*,
includes all the wild
cabbage-like
greens (Brassicas).
Self-propagating,
grows abundantly
all over Greece,
especially in winter
and spring, but also
during summer as a weed
among cultivated crops.
It has yellow flowers that appear towards
the end of spring.

History It is cited as *lapsáni* by Dioscorides and *vouniádes* by Athenaeus.

Properties There are three types. The species with white flowers has a radish-like taste and is the rarest. The black plants are bitter. The commonest varities are sweet.

Uses Mustard greens are usually boiled as a salad. Tender shoots can be added to omelettes. The small plants that spring up as weeds in irrigated fields are considered tastier than the winter variety. In many parts of Greece the spring plants are boiled lightly and eaten as a salad with extra virgin olive oil and vinegar. White mustard greens must be eaten in small quantities because they can cause flatulence and intestinal pains.

Folk medicine Good for the stomach.

rocket
rocket-salad

Eruca sativa, E. longinista, E.vesicaria
Roka, azúmato

Annual green which grows in many
parts of Greece, even in cities
(it springs up in Athens to this day,
wherever there are empty plots of land).
History Theophilus calls it *euzomo*
(with good juice) and *epísporo* because
it can be sown many times a year.
Properties It has a distinctive peppery, sharp taste.
Uses: Mainly raw in salads, on its own or combined
with other vegetables.
Folk medicine Tonic, slight stimulant, stomachic.

sowthistle
milkweed

Sonchus oleraceus
Zohós, sónhos

A very popular green, with a sweet taste.
Annual, self-propagating, adapts easily
to any soil but prefers tilled fields. When it finds
fertile ground it grows tall, with tender broad leaves,
but on less hospitable soil it stays small, with thorny leaves,
and is considerably tastier.
History Theophrastus mentions it as *sonkós*. Dioscorides
refers to it as "*the very tender, edible sónchos*".
Properties A classic green, popular for its sweet taste.
Uses: Boiled as a salad, combines very well with
the bitter taste of the chicories. Raw in a salad combined
with other greens such as Centaury and Picroides Reichardia.
Folk medicine Tonic for the heart. Antidote to scorpion bite. Its juice/cooking liquor
has been used to treat illnesses of the liver and the lower digestive tract/hypogastrium.

amaranth
red cockscomb, prince's feather, pigweed

Amaranthus hybridus, A. viridis, A. deflexus,
A. retroflexus, A. hypochondriacus
Vlíto

Grows as an annual weed in summer,
in cultivated fields and vineyards all over Greece.
History Theophrastus mentions it as *vlíton*.
Properties A classic summer green, refreshing in taste.
Uses As a salad, with garlic, vinegar and extra virgin olive oil,
alone or combined with other greens. Also casseroled with potatoes.
Folk medicine Styptic, good against diarrhoea, to wash ulcerous
sores, and more.

bryony
red bryony, cretan bryony

Bryonia cretica, B. dioica
*Avronía, vrionía, ovriá, aghrióklima (wild vine),
ambelurídha (of a vineyard)*

The plant that loves climbing up trees, shrubs and
bushes. Self-propagating perennial wild vine. It is mainly
encountered in gullies, gorges and places that have water,
in many parts of Greece.
History Ancient Greek references such as *i ámbelos i aghría*
(the wild vine) by Theophrastus and the *ophiostáphilo*
(serpent-grape) by Dioscorides, as well as several
of the common names in Modern Greek, suggest the plant's resemblance
to grape vines. It is also listed by Hippocrates as an antidote to tetanus.
Properties Extremely bitter, bryony contains a toxic substance, in small quantities
in the tendrils and leaves, and in greater concentration in the berries and roots.
Uses From February to April, harvest only the tendrils (which resemble
wild asparagus) and leaves (not the berries or roots). Blanch in plenty of boiling
water to remove bitterness, discard the cooking liquor, and eat as a salad.
Folk medicine Regenerates the blood, diuretic, cleans the kidneys, expectorant, emetic.
Needs to be used with caution because it is poisonous when consumed in large quantities.

burr parsley
mediterranean hartwort

Caucalis spp, Tordylium apulum

Kafkalíthra, kafkalídha

History Theophrastus and Dioscorides mention
it as *caukalís*.

Properties Fragrant green, with a wonderful discreet
and refined scent.

Uses In pies, soups, salads, and added to cooked dishes
as a herb. In small quantities in raw salads for its uncommon
taste. Gather from November to April.

Folk medicine Diuretic, stimulates the appetite.

glasswort
sea saltwort

Salicornia europaea

Armiríthra, armíra, and other names related to saltiness

A summer green found mainly in seaside regions,
which contains up to 17% salt.

History One of the few greens not known to the Ancient
Greeks. The only mention is by Galen, who explains
that it was burned to produce sodium for the
manufacture of soap. As its English common
name suggests it was also used as a source of
materials in glass manufacture.

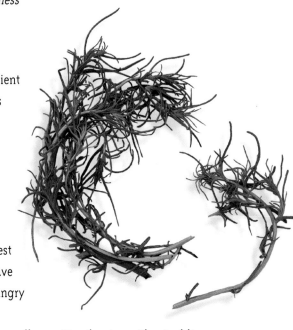

Properties A green with a rich full-bodied taste,
high in calories. Widespread in the inland parts of
Attica (Vravrona, Rafina etc), but unknown in the rest
of Greece with the exception of Crete, where they have
the saying "If you eat glasswort you shall not be hungry
all day long." Gather the tender shoots in summer.

Uses Eaten as a salad after being lightly boiled in a small quantity of water, without adding
any salt. It tastes best with vinegar but lemon goes well with it too. Can be eaten just like
Samphire, as its English common name suggests.

asparagus,
garden asparagus, sparrow grass

Asparagus aphyllus, A. officinalis,
Sparángi ághrio, aspárangos,
aghriosparangiá

Exquisite and valuable shoots.
Perennial thorny climbing bush
from which the cultivated asparagus is derived.
Found all over Greece in humid places
and river beds.

History Theophrastus
called it *asphárangos*,
Dioscorides a*spárangos;* both considered
it important. According to myth, Perigoune,
daughter of the robber Sine, was being chased
by Theseus, who wanted to make her his wife,
so she asked the gods for a hiding place. Then her dress got caught on the thorns of an
asparagus bush and she was transformed into one of its shoots.

Properties A choice food, with an excellent, crunchy, full flavour, more intense than that of the
cultivated asparagus. Rich in vitamins, magnesium and phosphorus.

Uses The tender shoots are eaten after removing the woody parts. Boil in salted water until
slightly soft, and eat as a salad. Combines wonderfully with eggs in an omelette, or with rice.
Gather from March to May.

Folk medicine Asparagus contains the diuretic substance asparagine which helps cells to
develop and renew themselves. Diuretic. A decoction of its root dissolves kidney stones.

wild garlic

Allium Scorodoprasum
Aghrióskordho

Globular bulbous root, biennial, self-propagating in many parts of Greece. Considered the ancestor of the cultivated garlic.

History Mentioned as *ágrion skórodon* (wild garlic) or *ophioskórodon* (serpent garlic) by Dioscorides and Hippocrates.

Properties Strong characteristic taste and aroma similar to the cultivated kind.

Uses Can be used widely just as the cultivated garlic. Those who love the taste use it in almost every savoury dish, from soups through cooked dishes to sauces and salads.

Folk medicine Important pharmaceutical qualities are ascribed to wild as to cultivated garlic. It is used to lower high blood pressure, to reduce fever and to disinfect the intestines.

stinging nettle
nettle, common nettle

Urtica dioica, U. urens, U. pilulifera
Tsuknídha (sting), knídhi (itch)

Annual weed with dark green serrate leaves, which grows over wide areas of Greece. All the parts above ground are covered in fine hairs which are full of an acid which causes pain and intense itching when touched.

History Theophrastus mentions it as *cnide* or *acalyphe*.

Properties It has a sweet, cool taste. It is very rich in Vitamin C. The leaves are rich in mineral salts and the tips contain calcium, copper, iron, sodium and potassium.

Uses Always wear gloves when handling it. The tender stems and leaves are boiled and eaten as salad. Also good in soups or casseroled, in pies and cooked dishes; it is better than spinach. The steam from nettles is recommended for deep cleansing the face. An infusion is used to rinse hair with dandruff or to prevent hair loss, or can be drunk as a tonic.

Folk medicine Nettle extract tones blood circulation and is good for detoxing, also for arthritis and rheumatism. Haemostatic, diuretic. Counteracts anaemia and diabetes. Compresses can be applied to acute arthritic joints, gout, sprains, and parts of the body with neuralgia, tendonitis and back pains.

centaury
century

Centaurea Raphanina
Alivárvaro, kentávrio, ververýda, karýda

Biennial, springs up in uncultivated land almost everywhere in Greece, with an impressive pale purplish-red flower with a thorn.

History This was mentioned by Dioscorides and Theophrastus as centaurion. According to myth, the centaur Chiron, teacher of Asclepius, used it to treat a wound Hercules suffered from a poisoned arrow; however when the wound did not heal Chiron was obliged to resign from immortality and cede his place to Prometheus.

Properties In the centre of the plant there is a thorn which has to be removed when preparing it. A relatively sweet green, with a distinctive taste. The strikingly beautiful mauve flowers are used to colour foodstuffs.

Uses Raw in salads, combined with cabbage or lettuce, or on its own in small quantities. Boiled briefly (3'-5') so it remains crunchy, with extra virgin olive oil and vinegar. The root of young plants can be eaten. Gather from November to April.

Folk medicine Digestive, tonic, promotes the appetite.

greater plantain
rat-tail plantain, waybread

Plantago major

Pendánevro (five ribs), arnóghlosso

Perennial, very common throughout Greece. Wide fleshy leaves with five distinctive veins or ribs radiating from the stem.

History Theophrastus mentions it as *arnóglosson*.

Properties Neutral smell, relatively sweet and refreshing in taste.

Uses: Combined with other greens, boiled as a salad or in pies. Needs to be cooked a little longer because it is fleshy.

Folk medicine Renowned since antiquity for its numerous pharmaceutical qualities. The leaves are diuretic, demulcent, haemostatic, expectorant and combat diarrhoea and diabetes. They also heal joint problems and backaches. The ripe seeds are cathartic.

samphire (krítamo)

samphire
rock samphire, sea fennel, St.Peter's cress

Crithmum maritimum

Krítamo, thalassóhorto (green of the sea), kríthmon

A green that grows near the sea, as it is aptly named. A favourite of those who live near the sea. Self-propagating, it grows on rocks near the sea, in many parts of Greece. It prefers inaccessible rocks, uninhabited islands and places far removed from human contact.

History The Ancient Greeks called it *kríthmon*, a name derived from the similarity of its seeds with those of barley (crithári). It was held in very high regard and held a place of honour in their cuisine.

Properties Its fleshy leaves resemble those of the olive, piquant with a slightly aromatic and salty taste.

Uses Eaten as a salad, raw or boiled, on its own or with other greens, also pickled. Gathered from February to August.

Folk medicine Tonic; purifies the blood. Contains minerals, iodine, essential oils and vitamins.

wild leek

Allium porrum

Aghriópraso, aghriokendanés, aghriokrémidho, ambelópraso

A miniature of the cultivated leek. Bulbous biennial, self-propagating, found in many parts of Greece, mainly in humid areas. The flowers are beautiful. It is the favourite food of the partridge, which digs up and eats its bulbous root.

History Probably the *ambelópraso* (vineyard leek) mentioned by Dioscorides. Held in high regard during the Byzantine period.

Properties Finer aroma and taste than the cultivated leek.

Uses: Whichever way it is cooked, it gives an excellent taste to pies and salads. Can also be cooked on its own, casseroled with tomatoes.

Folk medicine Antiseptic, tonic, rich source of vitamins, good for anaemia.

milkweed
common brighteyes
Picroides reichardia
Ghalatsídha, lagóhorto

Self-propagating annual, grows in many
regions of Greece, with distinctive woody
stems and small yellow flowers.
Not related to a poisonous green
(with a similar name in Greek)
belonging to the genus Euphorbia.

History It is listed by the Byzantines
as *galaktitis.*

Properties A green with a full,
semi-sweet taste, slightly astringent.
Its fragrance is reminiscent of milk,
hence its name in Greek (milk in Ancient Greek was
gála, pronounced *ghála* in Modern Greek, from
which comes the English words galaxy and Milky
Way).

Uses Eaten mainly raw in salads, but also boiled
with other greens, particularly bitter ones such as
the Chicories, and in pies. Gather from November
to April.

wild carrot

Daucus carota

Aghriokaróto, dafkí, stafilínakas

Fills the fields and the fallow land throughout Greece, even in open spaces in the cities. The common carrot was developed from it by horticulturalists in the 16th century. Tall biennial plant with impressive white flowers in distinctive umbels.

History Mentioned by various names including *daucon* by Theophrastus and *staphilínos* by Dioscorides.

Properties The leaves and the seeds are fragrant. The roots are white and smaller than the cultivated carrot but with a similar taste.

Uses Together with other greens, to add fragrance to salads and pies. The seeds can be used to flavour roasts and soups. Gather from November to April.

Folk medicine Tonic, diuretic, antiseptic. Sharpens eyesight. An infusion made from the seeds (whole dried umbels) is good for the kidneys. Used as a cosmetic against stretch marks.

salsify
oyster plant, vegetable oyster

Tragopogon porrifolius

*Skúlos, yéni tu trághu (goat's beard),
laghomústako (hare's whisker, moustache),
laghóhorto (hare's wort), musafíris (visitor,
guest), babakiá (cotton plant)*

Another tasty and relatively unknown green that grows everywhere in Greece. In Europe it is cultivated mainly for its taproot, which is large and plump. Biennial green with leaves similar to the leek, a stem with a slightly bitter milk, and an attractive purple flower. When fertilised, downy "feathers" form on the leaves (hence one of its common names in Greek, cotton plant).

History Mentioned as *tragopogon* by Theophrastus and Dioscourides.

Properties The white root, with its delicate taste of seafood, is particularly delicious. Care must be taken when pulling it up so it does not break.

Uses The tender leaves, shoots and roots are edible, raw or boiled, in salads and pies. When the roots are very large they are pickled. Gather from November to April.

Folk medicine Diuretic, cathartic.

artichoke
cardoon

Cynara cardunculus

Anginára me agáthia, kinára, káktos

The edible cactus. Perennial, self-propagating but also cultivated in many parts of southern Greece, particularly near the sea.

A winter vegetable, it blossoms in spring with an impressive purple flower which gives beautiful seeds.

History It must have been imported into Greece around the age of Alexander the Great, or earlier. Athenaeus refers to it as *cynara*, Theophrastus as *cactus*, and Epicharmus as *Sicilian cactus*.

Properties Pleasant fleshy taste, slightly bitter when raw, sweet when cooked.

Uses Eaten raw (in salads) with extra virgin olive oil and lemon juice. Cooked on its own or combines wonderfully with broad beans [fava beans], peas, carrots and potatoes. The tender leaves can be eaten and are tastier than the hearts. It can also be pickled.

Folk medicine Regenerates the blood. Was formerly used to treat malaria. A decoction of the leaves is good for the liver. It is effective against arteriosclerosis and high blood pressure.

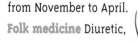

artichoke (anginára me agáthia)

french sorrel
curled dock

Rumex scutatus, R. obtusifilius

Lápatho, xinolápatho (sour lápatho), xiníthra (something sour)

A favourite green in northern Greece, particularly in Epirus. It is used in pies and cooked dishes. Self-propagating perennial with wide, undulate leaves. It grows in many places but prefers shady, cool spots.

History Dioscorides and Theophrastus refer to it as *lápathon* and *oxylápathon* (sour or acid lápathon).

Properties Pleasant slightly sour taste due to the potassium hydrogen oxalate it contains.

Uses Used instead of spinach in salads, cooked dishes and especially pies (in Epirus the Sorrel/Dock pie is widespread).

Gather from December to April.

Folk medicine Tonic, good for anaemia.

However, due to the oxalic acid and oxalate salts it contains it should not be eaten in large quantities because it irritates kidneys and rheumatism.

fennel
sweet fennel, and florence fennel [finocchio] (the bulb)

Foeniculum vulgare, F. officinale

Máratho, finókio, aghriomáratho, amarathiá, málathro

Biennial or perennial, fragrant green with an erect stem, yellow flowers on large umbels with smooth rays. Flourishes in infertile, dry areas almost everywhere in Greece as well as the other Mediterranean countries.

History Well-known and well-loved since antiquity. Theophrastus mentions it as *márathron* and *márathon*. The Ancient Greeks considered it a symbol of success, while the Romans loved it and used it a great deal in their cuisine.

Properties A wonderful sweet green, an intense, strong aroma that tends to overpower the other tastes in whatever dish it is added to.

Uses Widely used herb, in salads, pies, pulses, 'oily dishes', sauces and seafood. Fennel seeds are traditionally used to flavour olives and bread. The bulbous stalk base [finocchio] of cultivated Fennel (Foeniculum vulgare dulce) is sliced and eaten as a salad, dipped in batter and fried, or baked on its own or with cheese. Infused seeds are used to rinse the mouth after a meal. The essential oil of the seeds is used to make various liqueurs.
Gather the leaves, the tender shoots and the white root in winter and spring.

Folk medicine Fennel contains Vitamin C and A, iron, potassium and calcium. Tonic, digestive, expectorant.
Helps with problems of the urinary system.
Also heals various eye diseases.
Galactagogue (increases the milk flow of breastfeeding mothers).

κάππαρη

caper
caper bush
Capparis spinosa
Káppari

The chief appetiser of Greece and all the Mediterranean countries. Grows on beaches but even in cities, springing up from curbs and cracks in walls. Self-propagating perennial shrub with fleshy leaves and a very beautiful flower.

History Its name comes from the Ancient Greek *kápparis* (Theophrastus). Dioscorides gives a detailed description in which he confuses the seed with the bud, a common mistake to this day.

caper buds

caper shoots

Properties A characteristic aromatic and sharp taste which acts to stimulate the appetite.

Uses Eat just as in antiquity, in salads and sauces. The edible parts of the plant are the buds before the flowers open (what is generally known as capers), the tender shoots (which many consider tastier) and its oval seeds. Remove bitterness for 4-5 days with water or salt before eating. Can be eaten raw but more often is pickled (in vinegar or brine) to preserve for months. Rinse before eating to remove the strong taste of the vinegar or brine. Gather between January and July.

You can find recipes with capers on pages: 104, 107, 124, 133, 134 & 166.

Folk medicine Fights kidney infections, arteriosclerosis, the common cold, haemorrhoids and backache. Also a diuretic and a tonic.

caper shoots

caper seed pods

caper (káppari)
on a beach of Kea island

hyacinth bulb

Muscari comosum

*Volví, askordhuláki, kremidhúla (little onion), to psomí tu kuku
(cuckoo's bread)*

Perennial root bulb, under the earth, which resembles onions. The base of the bulb is flat with roots growing from it. It is found throughout Greece. The flower is purple or white, with matching coloured bulbs. It blossoms in spring, which is when it is gathered.

History The Ancient Greeks called them *volvoí* which is their spelling to this day in Modern Greek (though the pronunciation has changed) and is recognisably the origin of the English word 'bulb'.

Dioscorides praises bulbs as a tasty and nutritious food. The bucolic poet Theocritus mentions them as a necessary component of a peasant lunch, along with snails and a little good wine. Aristophanes ascribes aphrodisiac qualities to bulbs.

Properties Intensely bitter, spicy taste.

Uses Peel off the outer skin as you would an onion, then remove the bitterness by soaking in many changes of water. An excellent appetiser, dressed with vinegar and extra virgin olive oil. On Crete the purple flowers (called kavyús) are cooked with eggs in an omelette.

Folk medicine Diuretic, laxative.

common mallow

Malva sylvestris
Molóha, maláhi

Usually perennial, occasionally biennial. Bears large (up to 4cm diameter) pinkish-violet flowers from May to September. One of the most common greens in Greece, like the nettle, whose sting it soothes.

History Known in antiquity as *maláhe*, which is derived from the Ancient Greek word *áltho* which means 'to heal', this plant has been used since the time of Ancient Egypt. The Romans considered it a delicacy but also ascribed important pharmaceutical qualities to it. Pliny said that "a handful of Mallow a day keeps the doctor away".

Properties A refreshing, sweet, moist taste.

Uses The tender tips and leaves are eaten.

Folk medicine An important demulcent.

The flowers are expectorant and demulcent.

They relieve and heal bronchial upsets such as bronchitis and cough, and are used in manufacturing cough syrups.

basil
sweet basil
Ocimum basilicum

Vasilikós (royal, kingly)

The favourite plant in Greek
yards and balconies, very
widespread, grown in pots
and empty olive oil tins.
It is considered holy in Greece,
because according to tradition it sprang up
at the spot where lay buried the cross on which
Jesus Christ had been crucified, and its fragrance
led Saint Helen to discover the cross. Encountered
in many varieties, such as broad-leaved, curly,
small-leaved, forty-leaved. An annual (it dries up in winter)
with small white flowers in summer, which produce small
black seeds.

History Basil originated in India (where a related plant,
Ocimum sanctum L, is considered holy by the Hindus) but
came to Europe a very long time ago.

Properties Intensely fragrant plant, with a sweet taste with
slightly bitter undertones. Repels mosquitoes from the area
where it grows.

Uses A seasoning for vegetables, it goes particularly well with
tomatoes. Cosmetic use in the bath to relax the body. In
aromatherapy the essential oil is used for a stimulating
massage against depression.

Folk medicine Mild antiseptic and sedative. Antidepressant,
emetic, tonic, reduces fever, decongestant.   Soothes
headaches and itches. An extract from the leaves is beneficial
for the intestines and against vertigo.

golden thistle

Scolymus hispanicus

*Askolímbra, skólimos, skólimbros, skóliandros, asprágathos
(white thorn)*

A thorny plant that grows up to 80 cm tall. Found mainly in
southern Greece, abundant in cultivated fields. One of the
most beloved edible wild greens on Crete.

History Mentioned as *skólymos* by Dioscorides and Theophrastus.

Properties Difficult to cut because of its thorns, it must be
uprooted. Gathered from January to April.

Uses Eaten with its root, which is delicious. Boiled, roasted or
cooked with eggs in an omelette.

Folk medicine Diuretic, helpful with kidney stones.

Bay tree (dháfni apollonía) on the banks of the River Lúsio (Arcadia)

bay tree
sweet bay, sweet laurel

Laurus nobilis

Dháfni apollonía, váyia

The holy evergreen bush-tree. Very widespread in Greece and the other Mediterranean countries, self-propagating, mainly grows in places with sufficient moisture. In suitable soil it can become a tree and grow to heights of 10-15 m. The leaves are dark green, fragrant. The small pale yellowish flowers appear all at once.

History The Ancient Greeks crowned the victors of races with a wreath of bay leaves.

According to mythology, the god Apollo fell passionately in love with the nymph Daphne and pursued her. When he managed to grab hold of her, Daphne called out for help, her mother Gaia (the Earth) heard her and opened up to hide her. In her place sprang up the tree which bears her name. Apollo cut off a branch and crowned himself with it to comfort himself. Therefore in antiquity the bay tree was considered holy unto Apollo and was used to symbolise victory.

Properties The leaves and berries are fragrant and contain essential oil of exceptional quality.

Uses In cookery, as a seasoning in many dishes. A flavouring in some liqueurs. Pharmaceutical uses.

Folk medicine Bay leaves stimulate digestion and are stomachic. They are decongestant, diuretic, antiseptic and sudorific.

thyme
common thyme, wild thyme

Thymus vulgaris, T. serpyllum

Thimári

This brittle shrub grows in barren, dry, rocky soil all over Greece. It reaches a height of 30 cm, with a woody stem, tiny leaves and small pinkish purple flowers that appear in June and July. These scent the supreme thyme honey.

History Theophrastus called it *thymon*. Dioscorides called it *herpylos* (crawling), referring to its prostrate growth habit, which is also the Latin name of one of the varieties, serpyllum. Pliny recommends it as an antidote against snake bite, and for headaches.

Properties Intense aroma with slightly bitter taste.

Uses Gather the flowers and leaves (but not the woody stems) in small bunches and dry in a shady, ventilated place. Culinary use to season salads, seafood and many cooked dishes.

Folk medicine Antiseptic, expectorant, tonic and febrifuge.

rosemary

Rosmarinus officinalis

Dhendhrolívano (tree incense), arismarí

Fragrant shrub, with blue-green needle-like leaves and pale blue to pink flowers. Common in many parts of Greece, particularly close to the sea, hence its Latin name ros marinus (dew of the sea).

History In the rituals of ancient peoples it symbolised marriage, love and death, therefore when young women got married they were crowned with wreaths of rosemary. In the Middle Ages it was believed to be a powerful protection against evil spirits. Putting it under the bed was supposed to keep nightmares away. Even today it is believed to flourish in the gardens of homes where the woman is the boss.

Properties Rosemary contains essential oil and tannins.

Uses As a seasoning in food. Cultivated mainly for its essential oil, which is used extensively in perfumery. Cosmetic uses include steaming to deep cleanse the face and strengthen the skin. A compress soothes swollen eyes. It is good for oily

hair, making it shiny, darkening the colour and getting rid of dandruff. It makes a reviving bath and a refreshing and deodorising footbath.

Folk medicine Antiseptic, diuretic, stomachic, sudorific, stimulates hair growth and fights diabetes. Applied externally in an unguent it relieves rheumatism and migraines, or as a lotion rubbed into the scalp it retards hair loss. Flowers steeped in wine tone the heart and strengthen vision. Improves blood flow to the brain and therefore concentration. Taken internally in small doses it increases blood circulation and stimulates secretion of digestive juices and bile. Caution: in large doses it can cause spasms and vertigo.

chamomile
roman, wild chamomile, sweet false chamomile

Matricaria chamomilla

Hamomíli, hamómilo (low apple)

Humble in appearance but a giant in pharma-ceutical powers, the chamomile is one of the most useful healing plants.

Aromatic annual with flowers resembling daisies and marguerites. It is also named *'the plant doctor'* because sickly plants in a garden are strengthened when chamomile is planted near them.

History The Ancient Greeks called it *melo chamai* or 'low apple' because it grows low to the ground and it smelled of apples to them. It has been used for centuries by herbal healers. Usually encountered in flower-beds. It must be gathered as soon as it begins to flower, preferably early in the morning.

Properties Contains volatile oils, flavonoids, valerian acid, coumarin, tannins, salicylic acid, azulene and glycoside.

Uses Use the dried flowers, mainly as an infusion. An outstanding tisane. Recommended for cosmetic use to beautify face, eyes, hair and the entire body, and to lighten fair hair

Folk medicine Anti-inflammatory. Relieves skin irritations, itches and insect bites. Against anorexia and dyspepsia. Soothes babies with colic or teething pains. Used in homoeopathy.

oregano

Origanum vulgare

rĭghani

The favourite culinary herb in Greece, with a distinctive fragrance. A brittle perennial hairy shrub, reddish, friable, with small white flowers. Grows on dry wasteland on mainland and island Greece. Oregano gathered from barren places has a higher concentration of essential oils, meaning it is superior in taste and aroma.

History In wide use since antiquity, Theophrastus called it *orĭganon*. The generic name Origanum is from the Greek words *oros* and *ganos* meaning 'mountain glamour' or 'joy of the mountain'.

Properties Intense distinctive aroma with slightly bitter taste.

Uses From July to September gather the flowered stems in small bunches and dry in a shady, ventilated place. When dry rub between the palms to keep the flowers and leaves, discarding the stems. Oregano is the favourite herb in the Greek cuisine, and is used almost ubiquitously in salads, soups, appetisers and nearly always with meats.

Folk medicine Tonic, expectorant, spasmolytic, sudorific. An infusion is drunk as a tisane in cases of diarrhoea. Chew it to relieve toothache.

sage

Salvia officinalis

Faskómilo, elelífaskos, alisfakiá, salvia

Small perennial shrub with elliptical velvety leaves and violet-blue flowers appearing towards the end of summer. Grows in rocky, cool places. Its Latin name *salvia* is derived from *salvere* which means 'to be in good health'.

History Known since antiquity, mentioned by Dioscorides, Aetius, Hippocrates and Galen, who speak particularly highly of it. The Ancient Greeks considered it holy and used it as a votive offering to Zeus.

Properties Pleasantly aromatic, slightly peppery and bitter taste.

Uses: Gives a pleasant taste to many dishes such as soups, sauces, fish and pies. Infuse the leaves for a tisane, alone or in combination with other herbs.

Folk medicine Very effective anti-sudorific in cases of excessive perspiration. Antihypertensive, cooling, stimulating, digestive, emollient, styptic, stomachic, emmenagogue, tonic. Useful in liver disease, against rheumatism, headache, migraine, sore throat, tonsillitis and dyspepsia, and assists healing of wounds. A natural antibiotic. Leaves rubbed on teeth and gums have an antiseptic and cleansing action. Cosmetic uses include oily skin, pimples and acne, as a mask to deep-cleanse the skin, and as a steam bath. Is reputed to restore weakened memory. Must not be taken by epileptics, because it contains thujone which triggers epileptic attacks. Must also be avoided by breastfeeding mothers because it reduces lactation.

mountain 'tea'

Sideritis siriaca

*Tsái tu vunú (tea of the mountain), malotíra,
kolokimithiá*

Not a true tea, which is of the genus Thea or
Camellia.

Very widespread and popular tisane in Greece, it
loves high altitudes and rocky mountains.

On Crete its name is *malotíra* which is derived from
the Italian words *male tira* (that which draws out
illness), because the Venetians who occupied
Crete for some time found it a panacea,
particularly effective for the common cold and
respiratory problems.

History Its Latin name is from the name *sideritis*
(iron-ite) which Dioscorides used because the
plant supposedly healed wounds from iron
objects. Another explanation of the word is from
the pointy flower calyx which resembles the blade
of a lance.

Properties Pleasantly fragrant.

Uses The parts of the plant that are mainly used
are the leaves and the flowers, which must be
gathered while in bloom, around the middle of
summer. Infused or decocted and drunk as a
tisane.

Folk medicine Digestive, warming, tonic, detoxing. Recommended against the common cold,
illnesses of the respiratory system and the urinary
system.

spearmint, wild mint
garden mint, pea mint

Mentha spicata, M.pulegium

Ménta, dhiósmos

Perennial plant with some 30 varieties, among which spearmint, which is not so strong in taste as some of the others. It grows in many regions of southern Greece, particularly where there is running water. It looks like a thick shrub. Leaves are lanceolate and edges deeply serrate. Flowers are pale lilac, on spear-shaped spikes (hence both the Latin specific name and the English common name), and appear in July.

History Minthe was a nymph in Hades and Pluto's mistress. Persephone in a jealous rage tore her apart and Pluto transformed her into the herb that bears her name.

Properties A cool taste, due to the menthol it contains, and a pleasant aroma.

Uses As a tisane and in many dishes as a seasoning.

Folk medicine Good digestive. Antispasmodic, tonic, relaxes the blood vessels. In high dosages is analgesic and tranquilliser. Its cooling action soothes skin problems, fever, headache and migraine. Antibacterial, can help fight infection. Inhaled, it relieves a stuffy nose.

*wild mint
(ágria ménta)*

spearmint (dhiósmos)

bread

Psomí

The food which holds a special place in the history of the western world is bread. (Psomí)

The devotion shown by people throughout the ages, regardless of their religion, towards their Daily Bread shows us the great importance it had and continues to have for their survival.

In Ancient Greece, and even until recently in rural Greece, each family's needs for wheat, barley and other cereals were supplied mainly by their own production, which covered the entire cycle from sowing, harvesting, threshing to taking the grain to be ground into flour in the watermills or windmills that have now fallen into ruined disuse. The dough was always kneaded by the women and baked in the house's outdoor wood-fuelled oven, usually making enough bread in one batch to cover the family's needs for a fortnight. Every region of Greece had its own special breads which were connected with customs and traditions relating to milestones in life from birth to death.

Bread is often made in the small hours of the morning, when the rest of the household is still asleep, so the housewife can devote her full attention to this important task. Making traditional bread with sourdough is a ritual which starts by selecting the suitable wheat, and continues through sifting the flour to making the "sponge" with the sourdough starter from the previous night. Then the dough is kneaded thoroughly and covered with a blanket to keep it warm while it rises, and finally the loaves are baked in a hot oven. A portion of the dough is kept aside to serve as the starter for the next batch of bread.

This firm, solid bread stays fresh even after several days and has a characteristic pleasant smell and taste, due to the lactic acid it contains. Nowadays you can rarely find genuine sourdough bread because it is time-consuming to make and cannot be mass-produced. Yeast, which for practical reasons has become the main raising agent in commercial bakeries, makes a quick easy bread that is soft and fluffy when fresh, but quickly goes stale and is unappetising when only a day old. Sourdough bread is much better because it gives a longer feeling of satiety and has a lower glycaemic index, which means it does not raise the levels of blood glucose so suddenly.

A medium slice of bread with each of our main meals (breakfast, lunch, dinner) gives us about 250 calories.

RECIPE FOR SOURDOUGH STARTER
Prozími

- 500-600g flour (preferably wholemeal)
- 300-400ml lukewarm water
- ½ cup lemon juice
- 1 tsp salt

1 Thoroughly knead 250g flour, the lemon juice and the salt and leave the dough, covered, for 24 hours at room temperature.

2 After 24 hours add 125g flour and 100ml lukewarm water to the mixture, knead it well and leave it, covered, for another 24 hours at room temperature.

3 Repeat Step 2 on the third day. After the third 24 hour period the dough should have risen noticeably, which means it has become sourdough. If not, repeat Step 2 again and leave for another day.

4 The sourdough starter can be kept in the refrigerator up to 8 days, and in the freezer for several weeks.

5 If you do not make bread regularly, feed your starter once a week with 125g flour and 100ml lukewarm water.

SOURDOUGH BREAD

Psomí me pozimi

Breadmaking requires a good mood and patience. Hard white wheat flour results in the lightest bread, with an elastic dough that is easy to shape. Wholemeal wheat flour and mixed-grain (with seeds and whole grains) are not quite as light but still knead up well and give us a hearty bread. Yellow cornmeal and rye and barley flours lack the gluten of wheat so the dough will be less elastic and the bread will not rise as much, but it will still be delicious. The addition of a little soy flour or milk powder will help.

- 1 kg sourdough starter
- 1,200ml lukewarm water
- 900g hard white wheat flour
- 600g other flour, a selection or combination of: wholemeal wheat, mixed-grain, rye, barley, cornmeal
- 2 Tbsp extra virgin olive oil
- 1 Tbsp sugar (optional), 1 Tbsp vinegar
- a little additional extra virgin olive oil
- a little additional flour, 2 tsp salt
- a little flavouring (optional-aniseed and powdered mastic gum are traditional in Greece, mixed herbs or seeds such as nigella, cumin or coriander are also nice).

1 Dissolve the sourdough starter in the lukewarm water.

2 Sift the wheat flour into a basin, add the other flour(s), make a well in the middle of the flour and pour in the sourdough mixture. Knead well for 5 minutes. Leave the mixture for at least 8 hours to rise. The best temperature to activate sourdough is 30-35 °C; below 30 °C it acts very slowly, while above 40 °C it dies. To have sourdough starter for your next batch of bread put aside 1 kg of the dough at this stage, and leave it for 24 hours at room temperature. Then store in the refrigerator for a week, or feed it or freeze it as described in Steps 4 and 5 of the previous recipe.

3 After 8 hours the dough should have risen. Add the remaining ingredients and knead until the dough is smooth, light, elastic and not sticky-add a little more flour or water if necessary. The longer you knead the better, over-kneading will not harm this type of bread, while not kneading enough could lead to failure.

4 Place the dough in loaf tins or a deep circular baking pan which have been lightly dusted with flour or oiled so the bread does not stick to them. Leave to rise for an hour or until doubled.

5 Preheat the oven to 200 °C and bake for 50-60'. When the bread has cooled enough remove carefully from the pan. Place upside down on the oven rack and leave it for 5-10' at 200 °C to form a crust on the base and sides of the loaf.

Olympos, Karpathos

CHRISTBREAD
Hristópsomo

For the major feasts (Christmas and Easter) Christ-bread is made in most regions of Greece. This is a traditional, enriched festive bread, with many variations, from the simple addition of aniseed to a very rich version, like the recipe below from Crete.

1,200g hard white flour
70g yeast
1 cup lukewarm water
300g sugar
½ cup extra virgin olive oil
1 cup hot red wine
1 tsp salt
1 tsp mastic gum, crushed to a fine powder
200g walnuts, coarsely chopped
200g raisins or currants
½ tsp ground cinnamon
½ tsp ground cloves
peel of two oranges, finely chopped
zest of two oranges
½ cup orange juice
a little additional extra virgin olive oil
sesame seeds
walnuts

1 Prepare the starter on the previous day by combining 250g of the flour, the yeast and warm water.

2 The following morning add 100g of the sugar, half of the oil and a little flour, knead well and leave it to rise in a warm place.

3 Add all the remaining ingredients except for the last three and knead very well to get a smooth dough-add a little flour so it is not sticky.

4 Cover the dough and leave it to rise for 1-2 hours in a warm place

5 Form the Christbreads into any shape you like and place on an oiled baking tray. Each region in Greece has its own traditional shapes, ranging from crosses to round loaves decorated with fertility symbols such as farm animals and snakes

6 Leave to rise again, brush with oil and sprinkle with the sesame and walnuts.

7 Preheat the oven to 200 °C and bake for 15', then turn the oven down to 150 °C and bake for 35-40' longer.

rusks

Paximádhia

One of the most characteristic foods of Greece, particularly on the islands, is the rusk [zwieback]. It is made more or less like bread, with soft and hard wheat flour and other flours such as barley and rye, but it is sliced and then baked a second time to dry it out, rather like a thick Melba toast. Its usual shape results from cutting a loaf of bread into slices of equal thickness. The barley rusk is often made in the shape of a ring or bagel, and some rusks are cut into small cubes called "morsels" *(bukiés)*. The rusk stays fresh for a long time under almost any storage conditions.

THE MAIN TYPES ARE:

1 Wheat rusk, made from 70% and 90% hard flour or wholemeal wheat flour.

2 Barley rusk or Barley ring, made from 70% and 90% hard flour and wholemeal barley flour.

3 Eptazimo (meaning seven fermentations) rusk, made from ground chickpeas and 70% hard flour. These are unusual in that they are made without yeast or sourdough: leavening occurs through the natural fermentation of the ground chickpeas

4 Rye rusk, made from rye flour and 70% hard wholemeal flour.

5 Oil rusk, made from 70% and 90% hard flour and olive oil.

Sweet rusks are also made in many regions of Greece.

yoghurt

Yaúrti

γιαούρτι

MIRACULOUS ELIXIR OF LIFE

Rich in nutrients (protein, calcium, vitamins), easily digestible, light, cool and refreshing, yoghurt is an excellent choice and deserves a major place in a healthful diet.

Yoghurt is one of the most ancient foods known to humanity. The Ancient Greeks called it a 'therapeutic substance' because of its many beneficial effects on human health. It is mentioned both by the historian Herodotus and Galen, the famous physician of the second century B.C. One of the most enthusiastic consumers of yoghurt was the scholar and naturalist Pliny, who lived in the first century A.D.

There are many theories regarding how yoghurt was first created. The predominant one holds that it happened in the Middle East during the Neolithic period. It was probably discovered accidentally when a container of milk happened to be warmed for several hours and set into yoghurt. The warm climate of that region offered a favourable environment for the yoghurt bacilli to multiply naturally.

It is odd that yoghurt was virtually unknown in Western Europe and the United States until the 1920s. In 1908 the Pasteur Institute in Paris carried out research into the problem of premature aging of Europeans, which led them to conclude that the vigour and longevity of the peoples who lived in the East was due to their consumption of yoghurt. Since then yoghurt consumption has become widespread, mainly through the stream of Greek and Middle Eastern emigrants into Western countries.

Yoghurt, thanks to the lactic acid it contains, has a mildly sour, pleasant taste and can be preserved for longer than fresh milk. The micro-organisms that yoghurt contains convert the lactose in milk into lactic acid, giving the milk a thick consistency and rendering the milk fat more digestible, and they also neutralise harmful microbes in our gastro-enteric system.

Yoghurt contains a high percentage of proteins, vitamins, minerals (mainly zinc) and calcium. It is beneficial for smokers and heavy drinkers, because it protects the mucous lining of the stomach. It is one of the most easily digestible, yet nutritious, foods one can eat when one is down with the flu, even with a high fever. It restores the balance of the intestinal flora and the mucosa of the mouth for those undergoing long-term treatment with antibiotics.

It strengthens the body's immune system. Yoghurt can be used as an excellent substitute for much fattier high-calorie foods such as cream and mayonnaise.

Today a large variety of commercial yoghurts is available, some with added fruit, honey, cereals, and with fat content ranging from 0% to 10%. These are mainly made from cow's milk, while the more traditional yoghurt made from ewe's milk has become less popular because of its sour taste.

GREEK or STRAINED YOGHURT

Many recipes require strained yoghurt, which is thicker, richer and creamier than ordinary yoghurt. This may be sold as 'Greek' or 'Greek-style' yoghurt. If this is not available it is very easy to make at home. For each cup the recipe requires, strain 2 cups of natural (unsweetened, unflavoured, without gelatine) yoghurt. Use a double muslin [cheesecloth] square or two large clean cotton handkerchiefs (doubled), join the four corners, tie and hang from the kitchen tap to drip for about two hours to remove the whey, until reduced by about half. For a small quantity you can use paper coffee filters in a funnel.

If you leave it to drain overnight (refrigerated in warm weather) you get yoghurt cheese.

HOMEMADE YOGHURT

Serves 6-8

• 2 litres full-fat milk
• 1 cup natural yoghurt

1 Bring the milk to a boil in a saucepan. As soon as it boils remove from heat, pour into a glass or pottery bowl, and allow to cool to about 40 °C.

2 Mix the yoghurt (at room temperature) with 1 cup of the boiled milk, then gradually add to the remaining milk, stirring gently with a wooden spoon.

3 Place the bowl in a place where it can remain undisturbed, cover with a lid, then a blanket, and leave it to set overnight.

4 The yoghurt will be ready the following day. Keep refrigerated.

dry soil tomatoes

ánidhra domatákia

LESS WATER MEANS MORE FLAVOUR...

On most of the islands of the Aegean archipelago, the hot dry climate, minimal water and sparse soil have over the centuries led to the development of techniques for cultivating garden produce without irrigation.

On this rough uneven land, where the earth has been terraced for generations, farmers manage to cultivate tomatoes, beans, melons, watermelons, cucumbers, okra and other produce, without watering the plants, even in the midst of summer. This produce, although small in size, is delicious and grows without pesticides or chemical fertilisers. The most popular are the cherry tomatoes, which with bread and olives are a staple rural snack. These are sown at the beginning of spring and harvested early to mid-summer. On their own as a salad they make a light refreshing meal, ideal for the hot summer days. They are mainly used to make a tomato sauce which will keep for the entire year after being simmered slowly and strained well. They are also sun-dried by hanging in sunlight, which dries them on the outside while they stay juicy on the inside (See recipe page 135).

harvest on Santorini

Tomatoes are a good source of Vitamin C and contain large quantities of citric and oxalic acids. Their composition encourages the kidneys to filter large quantities of the fat which is concentrated in the blood. They are also a major source of lycopene, which is an antioxidant and anticancer agent that fights free radicals

honey

Méli

FOOD OF THE GODS

Honey is produced by bees from the nectar of flowers, which the bees gather and transform with the addition of their secretions.

In Greece the abundance of the local flora and the variety of terrains create exceptional conditions for apiculture. More than 100 different plants contribute to a greater or lesser extent to a Greek honey. The composition, the quality, the organoleptic characteristics and the types of Greek honey vary from region to region, even from year to year.

In Greek mythology honey was considered the exclusive food of the gods and demigods. Zeus, for example, was raised on milk and honey. It symbolised abundance and joy. According to myth, it was Aristaeos who taught the art of apiculture to humans. The ancients believed that honey fell with the morning dew from heaven onto the flowers and leaves, from which the bees gathered it.

Honey was valued greatly and was an important element of the Ancient Greek diet. It was used to made their confectioneries. A common breakfast drink in ancient times was warm water mixed with honey.

The thyme honey of Attica was and still is especially famous. It is distinguished by its special, intensely aromatic taste. It is produced in June and July, when the thyme blossoms, in regions with abundant thyme plants, such as Attica, the Cyclades, the Mani and Crete.

Honey is one of the few foods that is consumed exactly as it is produced in nature. One unique advantage is that it can be stored indefinitely, while keeping its characteristics and beneficial qualities intact.

Honey is one of the most nutritious natural foods, rich in carbohydrates and about 180 different trace elements.

figs

Sika  σύκα

THE PERENNIALLY ADORED FLOWER-FRUIT

The fig is one of the greatest delicacies to have accompanied humans throughout history. There was a fig tree in the Garden of Eden, and figs are mentioned many times in the Bible and in Babylonian hymn books dating to 2000 B.C. Figs are also mentioned by Homer in the *Iliad* and the *Odyssey*, as well as by Aristophanes and Herodotus. The Roman historian Pliny (52-113 A.D.) said, "Figs increase the strength of young people, preserve the elderly in better health and make them look younger with fewer wrinkles."

Ancient Athens and the surrounding Attica area were famous for their fig trees. The Athenian ruler Solon (639-559 B.C.) prohibited the export of figs from Greece, considering its inhabitants the only ones entitled to the fruit. During the first Olympic Games, the winners were offered figs as a medal.

Figs have a meaty consistency and contain numerous tiny seeds. When ripe they are rich in sugars and a considerable amount of carbohydrate. They must be eaten soon after harvest because they spoil easily. Their taste is sweet, reminiscent of honey.

When dried (Greek figs are dried naturally in the sun) they lose almost all their water content and can add a considerable number of nutritious calories to our diet throughout the year.

Figs are fat-free; they do not contain saturated fats, cholesterol or sodium. They are rich in fructose, and give us fibre, beta-carotene, and a significant amount of folic acid. They allow us to satisfy a sweet tooth without compromising a healthful diet. Daily consumption of dried figs helps prevent constipation.

Figs can be eaten as snacks between meals, on their own or with walnuts, to provide a quick energy boost. They also go well with yoghurt, and this combination encourages healthy bowel function.

almonds

Amíghdhala

αμύγδαλα

HARBINGERS OF SPRING

The most cheerful image in winter is indubitably an almond tree in bloom. Long before all the other trees, the almond tree (Prunus dulcis (Mill.) D.A. Webb ROSACEAE) blossoms in January or February, offering us its beautiful pale pink flowers.

Careful observers may notice another unusual thing: the blossoms appear before the new leaves, and often coexist alongside green buds and old dried nuts.

The tree is hardy and widespread throughout the Mediterranean basin. The fruit is elongated with a fuzzy green husk covering a hard shell which contains one or two nuts. There are two types, the bitter almond (Prunus dulcis var. amara (DC) Buckheim) and the sweet almond (Prunus dulcis var. dulcis (DC) Buckheim). Known since antiquity, it is mentioned by Dioscorides and Theophrastus. It was introduced to Europe by the Greeks, and the Romans called them Nuces graecae or Greek Nuts.

Almonds are an excellent source of protein and calcium and a valuable source of these nutrients for vegetarians and vegans. Sweet almond oil is used in cosmetics and for massage. Almonds are used widely in confectionery, cookery, to make drinks and pharmaceuticals.

In Greece they are used mainly by pastry cooks. Almond paste sweetmeats are the most important traditional sweets of the Aegean islands. Almonds are used widely in many desserts, raw or toasted, blanched or not, on their own or combined with walnuts in pastries such as baklavá, kataáfi, etc. Ground almonds are the base for orgeat (*sumádha*), a sweet cool drink made in many parts of Greece, and traditionally served at weddings on Crete.

walnuts

Karídhia κарύδια

THE APHRODISIACS

The tall, very long-lived walnut tree (Juglanus regia) grows in mountainous regions. Of Persian origin according to Pliny, it was called *káryon* by Theophrastus. The Latin name Juglans comes from Jovis glans, the nut of Jove (Jupiter, Zeus), after the ancient belief that the gods ate walnuts, while regia means royal, referring to its attractive appearance and its importance as a source of timber and food. Its fruit is egg-shaped or spherical, with a leathery exterior husk and a hard endocarp that contains the nut meat.

In Greece walnuts are used widely in confectionery and in cooking. Walnuts contain calcium, cobalt, manganese and iron. According to recent research walnuts decrease the incidence of cardiovascular disease as they reduce potentially harmful serum cholesterol levels.

Walnuts also increase sexual desire and stimulation. They contain polyunsaturated fatty acids which are beneficial to the blood clotting mechanism and the regulation of cardiac frequency. Walnuts are rich in fatty substances and should replace the saturated fats in foods such as butter and cakes. People who eat a lot of walnuts should watch their total fat and calorie intake.

sesame, tahini halva, pasteli

Susámi, tahíni, halvás, pastéli

σουσάμι

ταχίνι

χαλβάς

παστέλι

What makes these products so unique that their praises have been sung by all ancient civilisations? Why are they considered a traditional health food by Greeks?

The sesame seed was one of the first oil-bearing plants cultivated by humans. The plant originated in East Africa and was cultivated in most tropical, sub-tropical and southern regions of the world, including Greece. The use and cultivation of sesame is mentioned in many Ancient Greek texts, by Herodotus, Aristophanes and others. Hippocrates and Galen used it as a medicine. A mixture of tahini and honey, a kind of sesame-honey bar, was offered to the guests at weddings in Ancient Greece as a symbol of fertility.

Sesame seeds, tahini (the oily, creamy paste of ground sesame seeds) and sesame oil are all high-protein foods, especially rich in calcium, iron and phosphorus, and containing potassium, magnesium, zinc, selenium and certain amino acids lacking in other plant foods. They also contain unsaturated fatty acids that contribute towards a significant reduction in cholesterol. Tahini is known in many Middle Eastern countries and appears in many traditional main dishes, soups and appetisers.

Halvas is made from 60% tahini and a mixture of sugars, and is available plain, with almonds, cocoa or honey. It is an ideal

sesame seeds (above left), halvas (above right
pasteli (bottom left), tahini (bottom right

food, traditionally eaten by Greeks during their religious fasts, when the body is detoxifying and requires pure foods which supply quick energy and great nutritional value. It can also be eaten as a dessert, with cinnamon and lemon juice.

The sesame-honey bar (pastéli) is a traditional Greek sweetmeat made of sesame seeds and honey, which was a common treat in antiquity. Its ancient name was *sesamís* which it retained until the Byzantine era. Today this sweetmeat is made on many Aegean islands and in the Mani, and the ancient custom of serving it at weddings continues.

CRUNCHY SESAME-HONEY BAR FROM SIFNOS
Traghanó pastéli Sífnu

Traditional sesame-honey bars are made from only two ingredients, sesame seeds and honey, and they are very simple to make. There are two types, chewy and crunchy, depending on which of the two ingredients predominates. Success depends on the quality of the raw materials, their relative proportions and how well they are combined. The recipe that follows is for crunchy sesame-honey bars.

- 500g honey (preferably thyme)
- 600g raw sesame seeds
- ½ small wineglassful of sweet wine

1 Heat the honey in a saucepan over gentle heat, stirring constantly with a wooden spoon.
2 When the honey starts to thicken add the sesame seeds and continue stirring. The longer it cooks, the more fragrant it becomes, and the longer it can keep without spoiling. Test to see whether it is ready by dropping a little of the mixture on a plate. If it does not stick to the plate, it is ready and can be removed from the heat.
3 Cover the surface of a large table, preferably marble, with the wine and pour the mixture out onto it. Move it continuously from all sides with a spatula until it starts to cool. Roll out with a rolling pin until it is the desired thickness and shape.
4 When it is completely cold, cut it into pieces.

sea salt

θαλασσινό
αλάτι

Thalassinó aláti

THE ESSENTIAL ELEMENT OF LIFE AND HEALTH

The advantage and the value of sea salt comes from its crystalline structure and the natural way in which it is gathered. Unlike salt that is mined, sea salt contains iodine, potassium, calcium and magnesium, making it an invaluable source of all the trace elements essential for good health.

Greece is a Mediterranean country whose sunny coastlines are ideal for the production of salt crystals. The most ancient method of recovering the salt from the sea is still used to this day. Rocks on the beach are splashed by the waves, filling small depressions with sea water, which is then evaporated naturally by the sun and the wind, leaving behind the salt crystals (sodium chloride).

It is easy to gather this salt, and worth the trouble, since it is not only free for the taking, but also especially valuable and tasty.

Unprocessed sea salt is considered the caviar of salts. Try it coarsely ground, especially on salads and fried foods, and you will be able to taste the difference in flavour. It is exquisite.

recipes

pring onions [scallions] and tomato

general tips
for the recipes

HOW TO PREPARE FISH AND CEPHALOPOD MOLLUSCS

To scale fish, hold by tail and scrape from tail towards head with back of knife or scaling tool. Trim fins and tail (optional).

To gut a fish, cut open the belly from anal vent to chin. Remove all intestines, inner organs (the liver of some fish may be eaten) and gills. With the tip of a knife scrape away all the blood from the backbone. Use salt to rub away any black skin in the belly cavity as this is very bitter. Rinse thoroughly.

To remove head and spine from small fish such as anchovies, sardines and needlefish, hold the fish in one hand, head upwards, grab the head with the other hand and yank it downwards. If the flesh does not come away clean in two fillets, split each fish in half first by flattening it open with the back of your thumbnail, starting from the belly cavity and pressing towards the tail, then carefully lift off the head and spine.

To prepare squid [calamari] pull the head and surrounding tentacles from the body, cut away intestines and eyes, remove the beak in the centre of the tentacles. Remove backbone (like a clear strip of plastic) and any remaining innards from body. Rinse thoroughly, cut body into rings.

For cuttlefish proceed as with squid, except the backbone is a large flat rigid cuttle-bone that needs to be cut out (caged budgies will love it). If the body is large, cut into pieces rather than rings. Fresh octopus needs to be tenderised by beating with a mallet or against a rock if you are on a beach. (Skip this step for frozen octopus.). Then turn head inside out to remove innards, remove eyes and beak, separate into individual tentacles and cut head sac into pieces.

TOMATOES

Peel tomatoes by cutting out the core and lightly scoring a cross in the skin on the bottom, then plunging in hot water for 10"-15", until the skin begins to curl away from the cross. Lift the tomato out of the boiling water with a slotted spoon, let it cool slightly or plunge in cold water to cool, and peel it by pulling away the skin, which should come off easily now. Then seed the tomato by halving it crosswise and squeezing the seeds out. Finally, cut the halves in slices, then dice or chop.

AUBERGINES [EGGPLANTS]

Aubergines [eggplants] can be bitter so it is best to treat them before cooking. Wash, remove the stems, then cut into slices or cubes as required by the recipe. Sprinkle generously with salt, then leave in a colander for about 30' for the bitter juices to be drawn out. Rinse thoroughly and dry before cooking.

GARLIC

The papery white skin can be removed more easily if you crush the clove lightly with the blade of a knife. Cut off the dark root end. If the clove has begun to sprout this is not a problem, though some people prefer to remove the green shoot. When using whole cloves, crush lightly to release flavour. For purée, force each clove through a special garlic press. You can avoid peeling the garlic as the skins will remain in the basket, along with a little of the garlic. There is also a gadget with a reversible blade that makes a very fine purée on one side, or cuts very fine slices on the other. This is more expensive but wastes less garlic and does two jobs. It is worth investing in either one of these.

HERBS

The most popular fresh herbs in Greek cuisine are dill weed, flat-leaf parsley and dark-leaf celery (a variety with small stems, not the cultivated celery with a thick pale stalk), and, to a lesser extent, spearmint and fennel fronds. These are all sold fresh in small bunches. Wash, dry and chop finely. The easiest way to do so is using a special knife with a curved blade and a handle at each end (called a mezzaluna from the Italian for half-moon), which is used in a rocking motion across the herbs on a cutting board, or by snipping with kitchen scissors, or of course by chopping with a chef's knife.

By far the most commonly used dried herb is oregano. Look for it in decorative bunches in some speciality shops. As you sprinkle it on food. crush it between your fingertips to release its essential oils. Rosemary can be dried or fresh. The plant is very hardy and can grow in a pot on a balcony. Fresh sprigs can be used instead of a brush to baste foods you are roasting or barbequeing. A sprig or two can be placed in a small bottle of extra virgin olive oil to flavour it, along with a few cloves of garlic and some chilli peppers if desired.

CITRUS ZEST

There are two ways of obtaining the perfume from well-washed citrus fruits, such as lemons and oranges. Either rub the rind of the whole fruit back and forth on the fine grid of a box grater, just two or three times on each spot, being careful not to grate too far down into the bitter white pith. This is rather wasteful as a lot of the zest will remain on the grater. Or use a zester tool and scrape it downwards against the surface of the whole fruit to remove the zest in fine strips that add a decorative note as well as flavour to foods. If the recipe also requires the juice of the lemon or orange, squeeze the fruit after removing the zest from the whole fruit. Otherwise, the peeled fruit will keep on a shelf in the refrigerator (not in the drawer or it will go mouldy) until the juice is required.

A 250ml (8 fl oz) measuring cup is used throughout.
A tablespoonful (Tbsp) is 15ml [about ½ fl oz].
A teaspoonful (tsp) is 5ml.

salads

Salátes

COS LETTUCE
[ROMAINE LETTUCE] SALAD　　104

SALAD OF RAW WILD GREENS　　104

POTATO SALAD WITH YOGHURT　　104

BEETROOT SALAD WITH YOGHURT　　107

CAPER SALAD WITH SAMPHIRE　　107

AUBERGINE [EGGPLANT] SALAD
WITH TAHINI　　107

PURSLANE WITH YOGHURT　　108

SUMMER GREENS SALAD　　108

SALAD WITH BOILED CHICORY
AND SOWTHISTLE　　109

SWEET RED PEPPERS FROM FLORINA　　109

RICE SALAD　　III

PEASANT SALAD　　III

potato salad with yoghu

COS [ROMAINE] LETTUCE SALAD

Marulosaláta

Serves 6

- 1 Cos [Romaine] lettuce
- 1 small bunch of rocket [arugula]
- ½ bunch of dill weed, washed and finely chopped
- 2 spring onions [scallions], washed and finely sliced
- 4 sun-dried tomatoes, cut into strips
- 3 Tbsp capers
- 150g feta cheese
- 2 Tbsp vinegar
- 1 Tbsp mustard
- 4 Tbsp extra virgin olive oil

1 Wash the lettuce and the rocket [arugula] thoroughly and spin dry or allow to drain well. Cut across into fairly thick slices, place in a salad bowl and add the dill and spring onion [scallion]. Toss well, add the tomatoes, capers and cheese.

2 Whisk the vinegar with the mustard and gradually add the extra virgin olive oil, or put all together in a screw-top jar and shake vigorously.

3 Pour the dressing over the salad and serve.

SALAD OF RAW WILD GREENS

Saláta me omá ágria hórta

Serves 6 — 8

- 1 kg various tender wild greens and shoots extra virgin olive oil (preferably freshly pressed)
- freshly squeezed lemon juice
- salt

1 Pick over and wash the greens thoroughly in many changes of water.

2 Drain and leave to dry very well or spin in a salad spinner. It is important that they dry well so they can absorb the oil better.

3 Toss continuously in a deep basin while gradually adding the olive oil, lemon juice and salt to taste.

POTATO SALAD WITH YOGHURT

Patatosaláta me yaúrti

Serves 4

- 3 medium potatoes
- 200g strained yoghurt
- 6 leaves spearmint, finely chopped
- 2-3 cloves garlic, puréed
- 2 hardboiled eggs, sliced
- salt
- ½ tsp thyme
- 2 Tbsp capers, rinsed
- 2 Tbsp extra virgin olive oil
- freshly ground black pepper

1 Wash the potatoes, boil in their jackets, peel and slice or dice.

2 Combine the yoghurt with the spearmint and the garlic.

3 Arrange the potato and egg slices on a platter, salt to taste, and while still hot pour on the cold yoghurt dressing and sprinkle with the thyme, capers, extra virgin olive oil and pepper.

Cos lettuce [romaine lettuce] salad

BEETROOT SALAD WITH YOGHURT

Patzarosaláta me yaúrti

Serves 6-8

- 500g beetroot (without leaves), boiled in skin, peeled and sliced
- ½ litre vinegar
- 250g strained yoghurt
- 2 cloves garlic, puréed
- salt

1 Marinate the beetroot in the vinegar for one hour, then drain.
2 Purée in a food processor, blender or through a food mill until smooth.
3 Mix in the yoghurt and garlic, adding salt to taste and a little vinegar if necessary.
4 Keep refrigerated and serve chilled.

CAPER SALAD WITH SAMPHIRE

Kaparosaláta me krítama

Serves 4

- 4 cups samphire (picked over and washed)
- 1 cup green olives, pitted
- 1½ cups pickled capers
  (shoots, flowers and seed pods)
- ½ cup extra virgin olive oil
- vinegar
- salt

1 Boil the samphire in plenty of salted water for 5'-6', and leave in a colander to drain well.
2 Pit the olives if they were not sold pitted, using a special tool if you have one (the one for pitting cherries will do), or cut the olive flesh off the stone with a sharp knife.

3 Rinse the pickled capers to remove excess vinegar and salt.
4 Arrange the samphire, capers and olives on a platter and pour on the extra virgin olive oil, adding salt and vinegar to taste.

AUBERGINE [EGGPLANT] SALAD WITH TAHINI

Melidzanosaláta me tahíni

Serves 8-10

- 3 large aubergines [eggplants]
- 200g tahini
- juice of 2 small lemons
- 2 medium onions, finely chopped
- ½ tsp ground cumin
- 100ml extra virgin olive oil
- 2 Tbsp walnuts, finely chopped with a knife
- 100g crushed zwieback or similar rusk
- 2 Tbsp flat-leaf parsley, finely chopped
- freshly ground black pepper
- salt

1 Roast the aubergines [eggplants] whole, directly on a gas flame, or on the element of an electric cooker, or over a charcoal barbeque, or under a hot grill [broiler] until the flesh is very soft. It does not matter if the skin gets charred. Leave to cool, then remove the skin and any seeds.
2 In a basin or food processor thoroughly combine the aubergine flesh with the tahini, lemon juice, onion and ground cumin. Gradually add the extra virgin olive oil in small amounts and keep mixing until it becomes a smooth paste.
3 Add the walnuts, as much crushed zwieback as necessary to absorb any excess fluid, the parsley and salt and pepper to taste. Mix lightly and serve.

eetroot salad with yughurt

salad of boiled chicory and sowthistle

SUMMER GREENS SALAD

Hortosaláta kalokeriní

Serves 4

- 500g small courgettes [zucchini]
- 500g courgette [zucchini] shoots (the tender tips of the courgette [zucchini] vine)
- 500g small potatoes, well scrubbed
- 500g wild amaranth
- ½ cup extra virgin olive oil
- freshly squeezed juice of 1 lemon or vinegar
- salt

1 Pick over the greens, wash and drain well.

2 Bring plenty of water to the boil in a large saucepan, then add salt and the courgettes [zucchini]. Boil for 10', remove with a slotted spoon and leave to drain in a colander. Then boil the courgette [zucchini] shoots in the same water for 5', remove with a slotted spoon and leave to drain in a colander. Then boil the potatoes in the same water for 10', add the amaranth and boil for another 10'-15'. Remove with a slotted spoon and leave to drain in a colander.

3 Arrange all the vegetables on a platter, pour on the extra virgin olive oil, and season with either lemon juice or vinegar. Add salt to taste.

PURSLANE WITH YOGHURT

Ghlistrídha me yaúrti

Serves 4

- 4 cups purslane (only the leaves)
- 2 cups strained yoghurt
- 3-4 cloves garlic, puréed
- 2 Tbsp extra virgin olive oil
- 2 Tbsp vinegar & salt
- 2-3 Tbsp crushed zwieback, Melba toast or similar rusk

1 Wash the purslane leaves and dry well.

2 Mix the purslane lightly with the yoghurt, garlic and extra virgin olive oil. Add vinegar and salt to taste. Finally, add enough crushed zwieback to absorb any excess fluid from the yoghurt. Keep refrigerated and serve chilled.

SALAD WITH BOILED CHICORY AND SOWTHISTLE

Saláta me vrastá radhíkia ke zohús

Serves 4-6

- 1 kg wild chicory and sowthistle
- ½ cup or more extra virgin olive oil
- freshly squeezed juice of 1 lemon
- salt

1 Pick over the greens and wash very thoroughly.

2 Bring 1 litre of water to the boil in a large saucepan and add the greens.

Boil the greens for 10'-20' until they are soft, without a lid if they are young and tender, or with the lid on if they are large and tough.

Remove from the saucepan with a slotted spoon and place in a colander.

Pour on 1 cupful of cold water to give them a bright green colour and leave to drain.

3 Place the required quantity on a shallow plate and pour on enough extra virgin olive oil to coat all the greens, then add the lemon juice and salt to taste. Serve at room temperature.

SWEET RED PEPPERS FROM FLORINA

Piperiés florínis

Serves 4-6

- 1 kg Florina peppers (a Greek variety, a fleshy, long pointy red sweet pepper (capsicum) [bell pepper])
- 2-3 cloves garlic, finely sliced or minced
- ½ cup flat-leaved parsley, finely chopped
- 4 Tbs extra virgin olive oil
- 1 Tbs vinegar
- salt

1 Wash the peppers and roast whole in a preheated oven at 250°C, or under a hot grill [broiler].

2 When the skin blisters and chars on both sides remove from heat and allow to cool. The skin will peel off easily then. Pull away the stem and scrape away the seeds with a spoon.

3 Place the oil, vinegar and salt in a screw-top jar and shake vigorously.

4 Arrange the peppers on a platter, sprinkle with the garlic and parsley, and pour on the vinaigrette.

RICE SALAD

Rizosaláta

Serves 4

- 4½ cups water
- ½ cup extra virgin olive oil
- 2 cups long-grain rice (for pilaf)
- 1 cup cucumber, diced
- 1 cup ripe tomato, peeled, seeded and diced
- 1 Hungarian wax pepper (called "horn" in Greek, a long pointy yellow-green, sliced finely
- 1 Florina pepper (fleshy, long pointy red sweet pepper (capsicum) [bell pepper]), sliced finely
- ½ cup flat-leaf parsley, finely chopped
- ½ cup capers
- ½ cup Kalamata olives, pitted
- 2 Tbsp vinegar
- juice of ½ lemon
- freshly ground black pepper
- 1 Tbsp mustard
- salt

1 Bring 4½ cups of water to the boil. Add 1 Tbsp of the extra virgin olive oil, salt and the rice. Boil while stirring occasionally for 10', then turn off the heat, cover the saucepan with a towel and leave to swell for 30'.

2 Combine the rice with the vegetables, capers, olives and parsley.

3 Whisk together the vinegar, lemon juice, mustard, pepper and a little salt for 2'-3', then gradually add the remaining extra virgin olive oil, beating continuously until they thicken, and pour over the rice.

PEASANT SALAD

Horiátiki saláta

Serves 4

- 1 kg firm, ripe tomatoes
- 1 cucumber, peeled
- salt & vinegar
- 1 medium onion
- 1 green sweet pepper (capsicum) [bell pepper]
- 180g feta cheese
- 80g Kalamata olives
- a good pinch of dried oregano
- 1/3 cup extra virgin olive oil

1 Cut the tomatoes into wedges or chunks, depending on size (not slices).

2 Slice the cucumber, onion and pepper.

3 Arrange in a bowl or deep plate, season with a dash of vinegar and salt to taste, and toss. Lay the feta cheese in a single slice on top, surround with the olives, sprinkle with oregano, and pour the extra virgin olive oil over all.

...e salad (left)
...asant salad (right)

soups

σούπες

Súpes

ek soup with egg and lemon (left)
ntil soup (right)

LEEK SOUP WITH EGG AND LEMON

Prasósupa me avgholémono

(Photo on p. 112)

Serves 6

- 1 kg leeks
- 500g celery including leaves
- ½ bunch fennel fronds
- 1 cup extra virgin olive oil
- ½ cup white wine
- 1.5 litres hot water
- salt & pepper
- 2 eggs, separated
- freshly squeezed juice of 1 lemon

1 Wash the vegetables very well, especially the leeks, which can be gritty between the leaves, and drain. Finely slice the leeks (white part only), and finely chop the fennel and the celery (with roots and leaves).

2 Heat the extra virgin olive oil in a saucepan, sauté the leeks with the celery until soft, stirring lightly. Add the wine, hot water, salt and pepper and simmer for 25'-30'.

3 Whisk the egg whites until stiff, add the yolks and continue to beat while gradually adding the lemon juice and a little of the hot liquid from the saucepan. Pour the mixture into the saucepan.

4 Shake the pot gently from side to side to mix the egg and lemon into the soup. Reheat very gently if necessary but do not boil or the egg will curdle. Serve hot.

NETTLE SOUP

Tsuknidhósupa

Serves 8

- 1 kg tender nettles
- ½ cup extra virgin olive oil
- 1 onion, finely chopped
- 4 cloves garlic, finely minced
- 2 Tbsp spearmint, finely chopped
- freshly ground black pepper
- ½ cup flour
- salt

1 Wash the nettles well (wearing rubber gloves) and blanch in boiling water for 2'-3'. Drain, reserving the cooking liquor, and chop finely.

2 Heat the olive oil and sauté the onion and garlic in a saucepan until soft. Add the nettle, spearmint, salt and pepper and mix well.

3 In a separate bowl mix the flour to a smooth paste with a little of the cooking liquor, then gradually add 1.5 litres of the cooking liquor.

4 Pour the mixture into the saucepan with the nettles, bring to the boil while stirring constantly to prevent lumps, and boil gently until thick. Serve hot.

trahanas soup with tomatos

TAHINI SOUP

Tahinósupa

Serves 6

- 2 potatoes, peeled
- 2 carrots, scraped and sliced
- 2 onions, peeled and sliced
- 2 tomatoes, peeled
- 2 courgettes [zucchini]
- 1 stalk celery including leaves
- 2 sprigs dill weed
- 250g orzo (pasta shaped like very
- large grains of rice)
- 5 Tbsp tahini
- freshly squeezed juice of 1 lemon & salt

1 Boil all the vegetables in 1½ litres salted water. Drain and reserve the cooking liquor.
2 Purée all the vegetables through the fine or medium disc (depending on the desired degree of smoothness or chunkiness) of a food mill, or wait until cooled and use a blender or food processor.
3 Bring the reserved cooking liquor to a boil in a saucepan, add the orzo and cook while stirring occasionally until nearly soft, then stir in the vegetable purée.
4 Dissolve the tahini with the lemon juice and gradually add some of the soup liquid while stirring continuously. Pour back into the saucepan and stir. Serve hot.

TRAHANA SOUP WITH TOMATO

Trahanósupa me domàta

Serves 4

- 5 + 2 Tbsp extra virgin olive oil
- 220g trahanas made from sweet milk
- 2 cloves garlic, finely minced
- 2 litres boiling water
- 2 Tbsp tomato paste
- 200g hard feta cheese, cubed
- paprika & salt

1 Heat 5 Tbsp extra virgin olive oil over medium heat in a saucepan and sauté the trahana with the garlic for 3'-5', stirring continuously.
2 Gradually add the boiling water and salt, and boil for 5'. Then add the tomato paste, stir well, and continue to boil for about 15' until the soup is thick.
3 Heat the remaining 2 Tbsp extra virgin olive oil in a small frying pan [skillet] and fry the feta cubes sprinkled with the paprika.
4 Stir the feta into the soup and serve.

CARROT SOUP

Karotósupa

Serves 6

- 6 Tbsp extra virgin olive oil
- 1 small leek, white part only, sliced
- 1 medium fennel bulb [finocchio], sliced
- 2 cloves garlic, sliced
- 700g carrots, scraped and coarsely chopped
- 1 Tbsp spearmint
- 1.5 litres hot water
- salt & freshly ground black pepper
- 200g straind yoghurt

1 Heat the oil in a saucepan over medium heat and sauté the leek, fennel bulb and garlic until soft. Add the carrots, spearmint and hot water and simmer for about 40' until the carrots are very soft.
2 Remove from heat and stir very well with a wooden spoon until the carrots disintegrate.
3 Season to taste with salt and pepper, add the yoghurt and stir lightly.
Serve immediately.

KAKAVIA (FISH SOUP)

Kakaviá

Serves 8

- 1.5 kg various small bony fish (fishmongers often sell a mixture for soups-see photo left)
- salt
- 2 potatoes, peeled and sliced
- 2 carrots, scraped and sliced
- 2 stalks celery, including the leaves
- 1 large onion, coarsely chopped
- 3 cloves garlic, lightly crushed
- 1 large tomato, sliced
- 1 cup white wine
- freshly squeezed juice of 1 lemon
- 1 cup extra virgin olive oil
- extra lemons

1 Scale and gut the fish, remove the gills, wash well and salt.

2 Arrange all the potatoes in a layer on the bottom of a saucepan, then the carrots, then the fish and all the remaining ingredients except the lemon juice. Barely cover the fish with water.

3 Boil uncovered over medium heat for 50'-55'.

4 Add the lemon juice, cover, bring to the boil again and remove from heat after 5'. Strain the soup and reserve the broth.

5 Work the fish through a fine drum sieve with a pounder or the back of a spoon to extract as much juice and flesh as possible. Discard the bones that remain in the sieve.

6 Purée all the vegetables through the fine or medium disc (depending on the desired degree of smoothness or chunkiness) of a food mill.

7 Combine the broth, fish and vegetables and reheat gently.

Serve hot with lemon wedges.

LENTIL SOUP

Fakés súpa

(photo p. 113)

Serves 6-8

- 500g green lentils (new season's)
- 3 cloves garlic, finely minced
- 2 ripe tomatoes, peeled, seeded and finely chopped
- 2 onions, finely chopped
- 1 carrot, sliced
- 1 stalk celery with leaves, finely chopped
- 1 tsp red pepper (paprika)
- 2 bay leaves
- ½ cup extra virgin olive oil
- salt
- vinegar
- a little additional extra virgin olive oil

1 Pick over the lentils and wash them.

2 Bring 1½ litres water to the boil, add the lentils and all the remaining ingredients, except the salt, oil and vinegar. Boil over a medium heat for about 30' until soft.

3 Shortly before removing from the heat add the extra virgin olive oil and salt.

4 Serve hot with a splash of vinegar and an additional Tbsp of olive oil in each plate.

Excellent accompanied by olives and rusks.

arious small fish for kakaviá soup

appetisers

Orektiká

omelette with wild asparag

raw artichokes with olive oil and lemon

RAW ARTICHOKES WITH OLIVE OIL AND LEMON

Anghináres omés ladholémono

Serves 4

- 4 tender young globe artichokes (spiky variety)
- 5 Tbsp freshly squeezed lemon juice (reserve the lemon cups)
- 1 clove garlic, puréed
- 1 cup extra virgin olive oil
- ½ tsp mustard
- freshly ground black pepper & salt
- additional juice of 1 lemon for the water (reserve the lemon cups)

1 Pull away the hard outer leaves of the artichoke, cut in half and remove the hairy choke with a knife or spoon. Rub exposed areas with the inside of the lemon cups as you are working. Finely slice the tender hearts and quickly drop into water with lemon juice so they do not blacken.

2 Whisk the 5 Tbsp lemon juice with the garlic until it thickens. Gradually add the extra virgin olive oil in a fine stream while beating constantly so it continues to thicken, then add the mustard and seasonings.

3 Arrange the drained artichoke slices on a platter, pour over the lemon and oil dressing and serve.

OMELETTE WITH WILD ASPARAGUS

Omelétta me ághria sparánghia

(see photo previous page)

Serves 4

- 8-12 wild asparagus, washed and dried
- 1 cup hot water
- 3 Tbsp extra virgin olive oil
- 6 eggs
- freshly ground black pepper & salt

1 Bring one cup of water to the boil in a frying pan [skillet], add the asparagus and the oil. Boil over a medium heat until all the water evaporates and only the oil is left.

2 Beat the eggs with salt and pepper, pour into the frying pan [skillet] and fry, using a wooden spoon to make holes in the omelette so the uncooked egg runs underneath.
Serve immediately as soon as the egg sets.

anchovies in lemon

ANCHOVIES IN LEMON JUICE
Ghávros sto lemóni

Serves 6-8

- 1 kg fresh anchovies
- 1 cup freshly squeezed lemon juice
- extra virgin olive oil
- ½ bunch flat-leaved parsley, leaves only,
- finely chopped
- 3-4 cloves garlic, sliced
- salt

1 Scale and gut the anchovies, wash, remove heads and spines.

2 Spread the fillets in a shallow container, salt and cover with lemon juice. Then refrigerate for 8 hours to marinate.

3 Drain the fillets from the marinade and serve topped with garlic slices, chopped parsley and a generous swirl of extra virgin olive oil.

For a different flavour, use vinegar in the marinade instead of lemon juice, although lemon is better if this dish is served with wine.

QUICK 'DAKOS' RUSK
Dákos svéltos

Serves 1

- 1 rectangular barley rusk
- 1 clove garlic, peeled but not crushed
- 1 small peeled tomato
- 1 Tbsp extra virgin olive oil (preferably "green", freshly pressed)
- a pinch of dried oregano

1 Wet one side of the rusk with water.

2 Hold the rusk in one hand, wet side towards palm, and rub the entire dry surface with the garlic clove.

3 Place on a plate, grate the tomato on top with the large holes of a box grater, and sprinkle with the extra virgin olive oil and oregano.

YELLOW SPLIT PEA PURÉE WITH CAPERS

Fáva me káppari

Serves 6-8

N.B. In Greek this dish is called fava, but is not to be confused
with the Italian fava, or broad beans [fava beans].

For the yellow split pea purée:
- 1 cup extra virgin olive oil
- 1 large onion, finely chopped
- 500g dry yellow split peas (preferably from Santorini), picked over very carefully
(they tend to have lots of tiny stones) and rinsed well in a sieve and left to drain
- 1.5 litres hot water
- 2 Tbsp lemon juice
- salt & pepper

For the sauce:
- 3 Tbsp extra virgin olive oil
- 1 small onion, finely sliced
- ½ cup white wine
- 2 cups tomato, peeled, seeded and finely chopped
- 100g capers (soaked in water for one hour)
- reshly ground black pepper
- salt

1 Heat ½ cup of the extra virgin olive oil over medium heat and sauté the chopped onion in it
until it softens.

2 Add the yellow split peas, mix and add enough hot water to cover to a depth of three fingers.
Leave to simmer over a low heat, stirring constantly, until the peas soften into a smooth purée.
From time to time remove the scum with a slotted spoon, and add more hot water if necessary.
Towards the end of the cooking time add the remaining ½ cup of extra virgin olive oil, the
lemon juice, and salt and pepper to taste. Cover the saucepan with a towel and leave to cool.

3 In the meantime make the sauce. Heat the 3 Tbsp extra virgin olive oil in a small frying pan
[skillet] and sauté the sliced onion until soft. Add the white wine, and when it stops sizzling
add the tomato and the drained capers. Simmer until the sauce thickens.

4 Serve the yellow split pea purée hot with a large dollop of caper sauce in the middle.

GARLIC SAUCE WITH WALNUTS AND SPINACH ROOTS

Skordhaliá me karídhia ke spanakórizes

Serves 6-8

- 500g tender spinach
- 4-6 cloves garlic, peeled
- 2 Tbsp vinegar
- salt
- 3-4 slices stale bread, soaked in water, then squeezed well to remove excess water
- 3/4 cup extra virgin olive oil
- 1 cup walnuts, finely chopped

1 Wash the spinach very thoroughly and drain well. Cut off the roots, chop finely, and reserve the leaves for another dish.

2 Pound the garlic with a little salt in a mortar and pestle or a mixer. When puréed gradually add the vinegar, the bread and the spinach roots. When it forms one smooth mass, add the extra virgin olive oil in a fine trickle, pounding continuously. If the mixture is too loose, add a little more bread.

3 Add the walnuts and mix lightly.

Serve with boiled beetroot

CUTTLEFISH WITH GREEN OLIVES

Supiés me prásines eliés

Serves 4

- 750g fresh cuttlefish (not very large)
- 1 cup extra virgin olive oil
- 2 medium onions, finely chopped
- 1 bunch of fennel fronds, finely chopped
- 1 ripe tomato, peeled, seeded, cubed
- 1 cup crushed green olives
- salt
- freshly ground black pepper

1 Prepare the cuttlefish, wash thoroughly, turning inside out, cut into pieces.

2 Heat the oil in a saucepan over a medium heat and sauté the onion until translucent.

3 Add the cuttlefish and fennel, cover and cook for 30'.

4 Add the tomato, olives, salt and pepper, cover and continue cooking over a medium heat a further 20'-25' until the cuttlefish softens and the liquid cooks away, leaving only the extra virgin olive oil.

arlic sauce with walnuts and spinach roots

AUBERGINES WITH PEPPERS AND YOGHURT

Melidzánes me piperiés ke yaúrti

Serves 4

- 3 medium aubergines [eggplants]
- 3 sweet red peppers (capsicums) [bell peppers]
- salt
- 2 onions, finely chopped
- ½ cup extra virgin olive oil
- 4 ripe tomatoes, peeled, seeded, finely chopped
- 2 sun-dried tomatoes, finely chopped
- 2 + 2 cloves garlic
- ½ tsp sugar
- 200g strained yoghurt

1 Wash the aubergines [eggplants] and peppers, dry and cut into 4cm strips. Salt the aubergines [eggplants] and leave 20' in a colander to drain (see p. 100).

2 Heat the oil in a saucepan and sauté the onion until soft. Add the chopped tomato, sun-dried tomatoes, 2 finely minced cloves of garlic and sugar. Cook over a low heat until the liquid cooks away and only the oil is left.

3 Rinse and dry the aubergines [eggplants] and spread in an oiled baking pan with the peppers. Roast in the oven at 180°C until soft, turning over so both sides cook.

4 Mix the yoghurt with 2 cloves garlic puréed in a garlic press.

5 Serve the aubergines [eggplants] and peppers on a platter, pour on the tomato sauce and top with the yoghurt.

GREENS RISSOLES

Hortarokeftédhes

Serves 6-8

- 1 bunch burr parsley
- 1 bunch tender daisy shoots
- 1 bunch dock or chard
- 1 bunch fennel fronds
- 1 bunch spearmint
- extra virgin olive oil
- 500g spring onions [scallions]
- freshly ground black pepper
- flour
- salt

1 Wash all the greens very well, allow to drain well, and chop finely.

2 Heat ½ cup extra virgin olive oil in a saucepan and sauté the onion for 2'-3'.

3 Add the greens, stir-fry for a few minutes, season with salt and pepper to taste and remove from heat.

4 When the mixture cools add flour and warm water, stirring constantly to make a thick batter.

5 Heat sufficient extra virgin olive oil over a medium heat to cover the bottom of a deep frying pan [skillet] to a depth of at least one centimetre [half an inch] then drop in spoonfuls of the batter and fry the rissoles on both sides until golden.

6 Drain and serve hot.

PICKLED BOILED HYACINTH BULBS

Volví vrastí tursí

Serves 8-10

- 500g hyacinth bulbs
- 4 cloves garlic, finely sliced
- 2 cups white vinegar
- extra virgin olive oil
- ½ bunch dill weed
- salt

1 Peel the bulbs as though they were onions, cutting off the root section at the bottom. Wash well and soak for one day, changing the water every eight hours.

2 Rinse well and boil over a medium heat in plenty of water for 5'. Leave in the hot water for 30', then drain.

3 Bring fresh water to the boil and boil the bulbs again for 10'-15' until soft, then drain immediately.

4 Salt the bulbs. Slice the garlic finely. Layer in a glass jar, adding the vinegar and enough water to cover. Pour on a little extra virgin olive oil to form a seal. They will keep for at least six months.

5 Serve by pouring fresh extra virgin olive oil and finely chopped dill weed on a plateful of the drained bulbs.

pickled hyacinth bu

'OWL' RUSK

Kukuváya

Serves 2

- 1 ring-shaped barley rusk (this looks like a large bagel)
- 3 Tbsp extra virgin olive oil
- 1 cup tomato, peeled and finely chopped
- salt to taste
- 200g 'xinotíri' or 'xinomizíthra' (tart creamy soft cheeses) or feta cheese, crumbled
- 1 Tbsp capers
- a pinch of dried oregano

1 Wet the barley rusk lightly with water until it is soft but not soggy. Split in half across (if it is not already sold split) and spread with 2 Tbsp of the oil.

2 Place the bottom piece on a plate, cover with tomato, sprinkle lightly with salt and half the cheese, place the other half of the rusk on top, add the remaining cheese, the capers, a sprinkling of oregano and the third Tbsp extra virgin olive oil. Or make two identical open-faced sandwiches, which side-by-side look like the big round eyes of an owl (hence the name).

SMALL OLIVE PIES

Eliopitákia

Serves 10-12

For the dough:
- 4 cups plain flour
- 2½ tsp baking powder
- 1½ cups orange juice
- 1½ cups light extra virgin olive oil

For the filling:
- 2 Tbsp extra virgin olive oil
- 4 spring onions [scallions], finely sliced
- 4 cups pitted black olives
- 1 bunch fresh spearmint, finely chopped

1 Prepare the dough: Sift the flour twice with the baking powder.

2 Combine the orange juice and the extra virgin olive oil in a basin. Gradually add the flour, mixing well to form a smooth dough. Divide into small balls and leave to rest, covered, in a warm place.

3 Preheat the oven to 180 °C.

4 Prepare the filling: Heat the extra virgin olive oil in a frying pan [skillet], add the onion and sauté lightly. Remove from heat and add the olives and mint, mixing lightly.

5 Roll out the little dough balls, place 1-2 Tbsp of filling in the centre, fold over to form triangles and pinch the edges together to seal. Continue until all the filling is used up.

6 Oil a baking tray, place the little pies on it, bake at 180 °C until golden, about 30'-40'.

"owl" rusk

octopus in wine and olives

PICKLED CAPERS
Káppari tursí

- 1 kg capers (tender shoots, flowers and seeds)
- 2 cups white vinegar & salt

1 Wash the capers well and soak for one day, changing the water every eight hours. Rinse.
2 Bring water to a boil, add a little salt, and blanch the capers for 2'-3'. Remove with a slotted spoon.
3 Fill a glass jar with the capers, add the vinegar and enough water to cover.
4 They will keep for several months.

OLIVE PASTE WITH FENNEL
Poltós eliás me máratho
Serves 6-8

- 2 cups black olives, pitted
- 1 clove of garlic, finely minced
- 2 Tbsp tsipouro or raki (a clear spirit similar to the Italian grappa)
- 2 Tbsp fennel fronds, finely chopped
- 1 Tbsp lemon juice
- 1 Tbsp vinegar
- freshly ground black pepper
- 3 Tbsp extra virgin olive oil
- a little additional extra virgin olive oil

1 Pound all the ingredients together in a mortar and pestle (or mixer at slow speed) until it forms a smooth paste.
2 Place in a jar, pressing down lightly on top, and pour on a little additional extra virgin olive oil to form a seal on top.
It keeps for a long time if refrigerated.

OCTOPUS IN WINE WITH OLIVES
Htapódhi krasáto me eliés
Serves 6-8

- 1 octopus weighing about 1 kg
- ½ cup extra virgin olive oil
- 1 onion, finely chopped
- 1½ cup dry red wine
- 1 cup pitted olives
- ½ cup fennel fronds, finely chopped
- freshly ground black pepper

1 Prepare the octopus (see page 100).
2 Heat a deep frying pan [skillet] or saucepan over a

low to medium heat, add the octopus pieces without any water, cover and leave it to cook in its own juices for 15', watching to make sure it does not burn.

3 Add the extra virgin olive oil and the onion, stir lightly for 3'-4', then add the wine. When it stops sizzling cover the pan and leave to cook for 15'.

4 Add the olives, fennel fronds and pepper and cook another 15'.

5 Remove from heat and serve at room temperature.

FISH ROE SALAD WITHOUT BREAD

Taramosaláta horís psomí

Serves 4

• 3 Tbsp white fish roe (called taramà; avoid the inferior kind that is dyed a bright pink)
• 1 small onion, very finely minced
• 2 cups extra virgin olive oil
• freshly squeezed juice of 1 large lemon

1 Pound the fish roe in a mortar and pestle with the onion and the lemon juice (or use a food processor at low speed) until it becomes a smooth paste.

2 Gradually add the extra virgin olive oil a little at a time and continue pounding or blending patiently until the mixture becomes homogenous and has absorbed all the extra virgin olive oil. Taste and adjust seasoning, adding more lemon juice if necessary.

Serve in small dishes, to spread on bread.

SUN-DRIED TOMATOES

Domátes liastés

• 12-18 small, ripe tomatoes
• coarse sea salt
• 5-6 spearmint leaves
• 2 cloves garlic, lightly crushed
• extra virgin olive oil

1 Wash the tomatoes and cut in half horizontally.

2 Place in a baking pan, cut side up, and sprinkle with coarse salt.

3 If there is enough time and patience place the baking pan in the sun all day long for 3-4 days until the tomatoes become dehydrated, remembering to bring the pan indoors every night. Otherwise put the baking pan in a 60-80 °C oven for about 6-8 hours.

4 Shake the dry tomatoes to remove excess salt, place in a wide-mouthed jar with the spearmint leaves and garlic and cover with the extra virgin olive oil. In this way they can be preserved for a long time.

5 They are an excellent meze, a titbit [tidbit] to accompany an aperitif such as ouzo. They can also be used to add wonderful flavour to salads and sauces.

pies

ΠΊΤΕΣ

Píttes

AN INGENIOUS IDEA...

Bread and food togethe can be eaten and carried about easily, a complete balanced meal in one. The Greek name for pie, 'pitta', is derived from the Ancient Greek word 'plakous' which was the thin flat bread common to that time. This name gradually developed into 'pissa' from the resin of pine trees, which as it drips forms flat pools reminiscent of the shape of the bread. When the Greeks colonised the south of Italy the 'pitta' spread to that region and became established as the name of the thin flat bread. In the local Italian dialect the word 'pitta' became 'pizza', which with its variety of savoury toppings is known worldwide.

Pies of the type encountered in Greece today likely developed during the Byzantine era.
They became established as a basic, almost daily food in the mountainous regions of central and northern Greece, because of the lifestyle there. Nomadic herders leading their flocks of sheep and goats to remote grazing grounds or farmers working all day in the fields needed a food that was easy to transport and eat.

Of course pies are known in all other regions of Greece as well, and vary accoding to the locally available ingredients, such as cheese, wheat, butter, etc. Epirus in particular is famous for its pies, and their creative simplicity gives cooks an opportunity to show off their skills.

It is important to note that although pies can also be made with commercial phyllo, the flavour does not compare with homemade phyllo.

BASIC RECIPE FOR PHYLLO

Vasikí sintayí ya fílla zímis

For 8 sheets

- 750g soft flour
- I level tsp salt
- 3 Tbsp extra virgin olive oil
- I Tbsp vinegar
- I liter warm water
- a little extra flour

1 Sift the flour twice into a basin.

2 Make a well in the middle and add the remaining ingredients.

3 Knead the mixture well, adding a little more flour or water if necessary so the dough is neither dry nor sticky.

4 Cut the dough into eight equal portions, roll into balls, and leave in the basin, covered with a damp cloth, to rest for I-2 hours.

5 Use a large clean surface such as an uncluttered kitchen counter, the kitchen table or a plastí ri, the traditional large round wooden board made for this purpose, Sprinkle the surface with flour or corn flour, flatten a ball of dough on it, and sprinkle with a little more flour or corn flour on top. Then roll the dough out with a rolling pin, until it is as fine as you can make it, and reaches the desired dimensions, sprinkling with a little more flour as needed.

quick pies

CYCLADIC OIL PIE

Ladhénia kikladhítiki
Serves 6-8

- 500g plain flour
- 1 cup warm water
- 2 onions, finely chopped
- 1 cup extra virgin olive oil
- ground pepper & salt
- 10g yeast or 1 packet instant dry
- a pinch of salt
- 3 ripe tomatoes, peeled,
- seeded and finely chopped

1 Preheat the oven to 180 °C.

2 Sift the flour twice into a basin

3 Make a well in the middle and add the yeast and warm water, with a pinch of salt. If using fresh yeast, dissolve it in the water first. If using instant dry yeast, stir it into the flour and then add the water. Knead well and leave the dough in a warm place to rise until doubled.

4 Oil a baking pan and spread out the dough to cover the bottom. Sprinkle the top first with the chopped onion, then with the chopped tomatoes, season with salt and pepper and cover the entire surface with extra virgin olive oil.

5 Bake for 40'-50' at 180 °C. Serve hot.

batter pie with pumpkin

BASIC BATTER PIE

Kasópitta

Serves 6-8

- 500g self-raising flour
- a pinch of salt
- 1 cup warm milk
- 3 eggs, beaten
- 1 cup extra virgin olive oil
- 400g feta cheese
- 120g yoghurt
- a few spoonfuls additional extra virgin olive oil

1 Preheat the oven to 300 °C.

2 Sift the flour twice into a basin.

3 Make a well in the middle, add the salt, and gradually stir in the milk, eggs and extra virgin olive oil. Crumble the feta by hand and add, reserving a little for garnish. Finally, stir in the yoghurt. The mixture should be neither runny nor dry. Adjust by adding a little milk or flour if necessary.

4 Oil a baking pan and heat for 3' in the oven. Remove, cover the bottom with a few spoonfuls of extra virgin olive oil and sprinkle with the reserved feta.

5 Bake at the bottom of the oven for 15' at 300 °C, then lower to 180 °C and bake a further 30'-40' until golden. Serve hot.

Variations on this basic recipe:

BATTER PIE WITH COURGETTE [ZUCCHINI] OR PUMPKIN

Zimarópitta me kolokithi

Serves 6-8

- 500g self-raising flour
- salt to taste
- 400g courgette [zucchini] or pumpkin, coarsely
- grated and left in a colander to drain well
- 2 eggs
- 1 cup extra virgin olive oil
- 200g feta cheese
- 1 bunch dill weed or fennel fronds, finely chopped
- a few spoonfuls additional extra virgin olive oil

Follow the instructions for the Basic Batter Pie.

BATTER PIE WITH SPINACH

Zimarópitta me spanàki

Serves 6-8

- 500g self-raising flour
- 1 cup extra virgin olive oil
- 2 spring onions [scallions], finely sliced
- 500g spinach, picked over, washed very well, chopped coarsely and left in a colander to drain well
- a little dill weed, finely chopped
- ground pepper & salt
- 125g yoghurt
- a few spoonfuls additional extra virgin olive oil

1 Take a little of the oil, sauté the spring onions [scallions] in a large frying pan [skillet] until translucent. Add the spinach, dill, salt and pepper and mix.

2 Sift the flour into a basin, add the spinach mixture, the yoghurt and the remaining extra virgin olive oil and mix thoroughly. Continue from Step 4 of the instructions for the Basic Batter Pie.

pies with a twist

AN INTERESTING TYPE OF PIE WITH A LITERAL TWIST, RELATIVELY EASY TO MAKE, IN WHICH THE PHYLLO EMBRACES THE FILLING

TWISTED LEEK AND CHEESE PIE

Prasotirópitta striftí

Serves 10-12

- 750g young leeks
- ½ cup extra virgin olive oil
- ½ cup spearmint, finely chopped
- ½ cup parsley, finely chopped
- 1 cup dill weed, finely chopped
- 1 tsp ground black pepper & salt
- 400g feta cheese or anthotiro, a soft mild white cheese (ricotta or cottage cheese can be substituted)
- 250g yoghurt, preferably made from ewes' milk
- 4 eggs
- ½ cup additional extra virgin olive oil

the ingredients for the Basic Phyllo Recipe
(see page 138)

1 Prepare one Basic Phyllo Recipe, dividing the dough into six equal portions, and leave to rest while preparing the filling.

2 Preheat the oven to 250 °C. Wash the leeks very well as sand can lurk between the top leaves, and slice finely including the tender green part.

3 Heat ½ cup extra virgin olive oil over medium heat in a deep frying pan [skillet] and sauté the leek until translucent. Remove from heat and add the chopped spearmint, parsley and dill, mixing lightly. Add salt and

Twisted leek and cheese pie

143

pepper to taste.

4 Crumble the feta or soft white cheese by hand into a large basin and add the yoghurt and eggs. Mix and add the mixture from the frying pan [skillet]. Taste and adjust seasonings if necessary.

5 Make six phyllo sheets as described in the Basic Phyllo Recipe. Then oil a 40cm diameter baking pan.

6 Gently lay each phyllo sheet on a lightly floured surface, spread some filling lengthwise and sprinkle with a little extra virgin olive oil. Roll it up into a sausage shape, about 3cm diameter, and twist. Then coil it in a spiral starting from the centre of the baking pan. Continue with the other sheets of phyllo, coiling progressively around the centre, until all the ingredients are used up. Brush the entire surface of the pie generously with extra virgin olive oil.

7 Bake in the preheated oven at 250 °C for 10', then lower to 180°C and bake a further 50' or so until golden. Sprinkle the pie with a little water halfway through cooking so it does not dry out. Serve hot.

TWISTED GREENS PIE
Hortópitta striftí

Serves 6-8

- 1 cup extra virgin olive oil
- 4 spring onions, finely chopped
- 1 kg mixed wild greens (dock, hartwort, wild carrot, fennel, nettle, etc), picked over, washed very well and chopped finely
- ground pepper
- salt

Heat the extra virgin olive oil in a deep frying pan [skillet] and sauté the spring onion until translucent.

Remove from heat and add the greens, mixing lightly. Add salt and pepper to taste.

Proceed from Step 6 of the Twisted Leek and Cheese Pie (see page 143).

TWISTED SPINACH PIE

Spanakotirópitta striftí

Serves 8-10

- 1 kg spinach

Pick over the spinach, wash very well, chop coarsely, blanch quickly and drain well.
Add to 250g sautéed leek (instead of 750g leek as in the basic recipe) along with the other ingredients of the Twisted Leek and Cheese Pie. Proceed from Step 2 of the Twisted Leek and Cheese Pie (see page 143).

TWISTED CHEESE PIE

Tirópitta striftí

Serves 6-8

- 400g feta cheese
- 250g yoghurt, preferably made from ewe's milk
- 1 cup extra virgin olive oil
- 7 eggs
- salt

Beat the eggs in a bowl, crumble the feta into it by hand, add the yoghurt, oil and mix lightly. Add salt if it needs it (taste first as the feta can be very salty).

Proceed from Step 6 of the Twisted Leek and Cheese Pie (see page 143).

TWISTED PUMPKIN PIE

Kolokithópitta striftí

Serves 6-8

- 700g pumpkin, coarsely grated and left in a colander to drain well
- ½ cup short-grain white rice
- ½ cup sugar
- 1 cup extra virgin olive oil
- ½ tsp ground cinnamon
- 400g feta cheese
- salt

Place the pumpkin in a basin, make a well in the middle and add the remaining ingredients, crumbling the feta coarsely by hand. Mix lightly but thoroughly and taste before adding the salt.

Proceed from Step 6 of the Twisted Leek and Cheese Pie (see page 143).

classic pies

TO SHOW OFF YOUR ADVANCED CULINARY SKILLS...

COURGETTE [ZUCCHINI] PIE

Kolokithópitta

Serves 8

- 2 kg fresh courgette [zucchini] or pumpkin
- 2 medium onions, finely chopped
- ½ cup spearmint, finely chopped
- 4 eggs, beaten
- 8 sheets phyllo pastry from **Basic Phyllo Recipe (page 138)**

- 1 cup extra virgin olive oil
- ½ cup dill weed, finely chopped
- 400g feta cheese, crumbled
- salt
- freshly ground black pepper
- some additional extra virgin olive oil

1 Preheat the oven to 250 °C.

2 Wash the pumpkin and peel it, or wash the courgettes [zucchini] and top and tail them, scraping away any brown spots. Grate coarsely and leave in a colander to drain. If using courgettes squeeze to remove excess juices.

3 Heat the extra virgin olive oil in a saucepan and sauté the onion until golden.

4 Add the grated pumpkin or courgettes [zucchini] and stir lightly until any liquid evaporates and it looks dry. Remove from heat.

5 Add the dill weed, spearmint, feta and eggs, season with salt and pepper and mix well.

6 Brush a baking pan with oil, cover with two oiled sheets of phyllo pastry, spread on a layer of mixture, continue in the same way with four more sheets, and end with two sheets of phyllo on top. Sprinkle lightly with a little oil and water.

7 Bake in the oven at 250 °C for about one hour until golden.

SPRING PIE WITH AROMATIC WILD GREENS

Anixiàtiki pítta me aromatikà aghrióhorta

Serves 10-12

- 1½ cups extra virgin olive oil
- 4 spring onions [scallions], finely sliced
- 4 wild leeks, chopped finely
- 1 kg mixed wild greens (hartwort, wild carrot, fennel, nettle, dock etc), picked over, washed very well and chopped finely
- 8 sheets phyllo pastry
- ground pepper and salt

1 Preheat the oven to 250 °C.

2 Heat a little of the oil in a saucepan and sauté the onion and leek until translucent.

3 Remove from heat, add all the other ingredients and the remaining extra virgin olive oil and mix lightly.

4 Place a 40cm diameter baking pan upside down on the bottom of the hot oven. Roll one phyllo sheet on the rolling pin (or the long thin wooden rod used as a rolling pin in Greece) and carefully spread the sheet on the baking pan to bake a little until it is a very light golden colour, then repeat for 3 more sheets of phyllo.

5 Oil the baking pan. Brush one sheet of raw phyllo with oil, spread on the bottom of the pan, repeat with a second sheet. Spread a layer of filling, two sheets of precooked phyllo, more filling, two more sheets of precooked phyllo, the remaining filling, and the last two raw sheets of phyllo, brushed one by one with oil.

6 Fold the edges of the phyllo over, brush the entire surface generously with oil and sprinkle with a little warm water, and bake on the bottom shelf of the oven at 250 °C for 30', then lower to 180 °C and bake approximately 30' longer.

SPINACH AND CHEESE PIE FROM EPIRUS

Spanakotirópitta Ipirótiki

Serves 10-12

8 sheets phyllo pastry from Basic Phyllo Recipe (page 138)

- 1 kg spinach
- ½ cup extra virgin olive oil
- 1 medium onion, finely chopped
- 300g leeks, washed very well and finely sliced
- 300g feta cheese
- 2 eggs, beaten
- ½ cup dill weed, finely chopped
- a little spearmint, finely chopped
- a few fennel fronds, finely chopped
- salt
- freshly ground pepper
- a little more extra virgin olive oil

1 Preheat the oven to 250 °C

2 Pick over the spinach, wash very well, chop coarsely, blanch quickly and leave in a colander to drain well.

3 Heat a little of the oil in a saucepan and lightly sauté the onion and the leek until translucent. Remove from heat, add the spinach, the feta crumbled by hand, the eggs, the remaining oil and the other ingredients, and mix well.

4 Place a 40cm diameter baking pan upside down on the bottom of the hot oven. Roll one phyllo sheet on the rolling pin (or the long thin wooden rod used as a rolling pin in Greece) and carefully spread the sheet on the baking pan to bake a little until it is a very light golden colour, then repeat for 3 more sheets of phyllo.

5 Oil the baking pan. Brush one sheet of raw phyllo with oil, spread on the bottom of the pan, repeat with a second sheet. Spread a layer of filling, two sheets of precooked phyllo, more filling, two more sheets of precooked phyllo, the remaining filling, and the last two raw sheets of phyllo, brushed one by one with oil.

6 Fold the edges of the phyllo over, brush the entire surface generously with oil and sprinkle with a little warm water, and bake on the bottom shelf of the oven at 250 °C for 30', then lower to 180 °C and bake approximately 30' longer.

fish, seafood

ψάρια
θαλασσινά

Psária, thalassiná

MONKFISH WITH LEEKS	152	BAKED FISH WITH HERBS	162
GOLDEN MULLET IN WINE	154	GRIDDLED PIKE	162
SARDINES IN VINE LEAVES	156	CUTTLEFISH WITH HERBS	163
SARDINE ROLLS	157	RED MULLET EN PAPILLOTE	163
BAKED NEEDLEFISH WITH GARLIC	157	BAKED TUNA WITH SAGE	165
GILT-HEADED SEA BREAM FILLETS		BOGUE WITH CAPERS	166
WITH CELERY	158	GARLIC PRAWNS [SHRIMP]	166
COD CASSEROLE	160		

red mullet en papillote before cookin

MONKFISH WITH LEEKS

Peskandhrítsa me prása

Serves 6

- 1 cup extra virgin olive oil
- 750g leeks, finely sliced
- 3 onions, finely diced
- 1 bunch parsley, finely chopped
- 1 bunch dill weed, finely chopped
- 2 sprigs dark celery leaves, finely chopped
- 2 ripe tomatoes, peeled, seeded and finely chopped
- 1 cup hot water
- 1 kg monkfish fillets, cut into portions (if using whole monkfish, use the skinned tails, and save the heads for an excellent soup)
- Vfreshly squeezed juice of 1 lemon
- freshly ground black pepper
- salt

1 Heat ½ cup extra virgin olive oil and sauté the leek and onion until soft.

2 Add the parsley, dill, celery, tomato and hot water with a pinch of salt and simmer for about 30' until all the liquid evaporates and only the oil remains.

3 Steam the monkfish fillets for 8'.

4 Whisk the lemon juice with the remaining ½ cup extra virgin olive oil, freshly ground black pepper and a pinch of salt.

5 Serve the fish with the leek sauce, pouring the lemon-oil dressing over all.

GOLDEN MULLET IN WINE

Kutsomúres krasátes

Serves 4

- 1 kg small golden mullet
- some flour
- 1 cup extra virgin olive oil
- 2 cloves garlic, finely minced
- a few leaves of rosemary
- 1 cup dry white wine
- ½ cup flat-leaf parsley, finely chopped
- salt
- freshly ground black pepper

1 Scale, gut and remove the gills of the mullet, and wash well. Season with salt and pepper and dredge in flour.

2 Heat the oil in a large non-stick frying pan [skillet]. Add the garlic and rosemary and remove when golden.

3 Turn up the heat. Fry the fish for 1'-2' minutes on each side, just enough for the flour to form a crust.

4 Add the wine, cover the pan with a lid, turn down the heat and cook for about 5'.

Serve immediately, sprinkling with the parsley.

sardines

Sardhélles

HUMBLE BUT MIRACULOUS...

Available fresh all year round, sardines are tasty, cheap, and considered the most beneficial fish of the Greek seas. They supply good quality protein and contain eicosapentoic acid, which prevents blood clots, and Omega-3 fatty acids, which reduce serum triglycerides and lipoproteins. Their edibe bones are a significant source of calcium as an alternative to milk products and especially valuable for preventing osteoporosis.

SARDINES IN VINE LEAVES
Sardhélles sta klimatófilla
Serves 4

- 1 kg sardines
- salt
- freshly squeezed juice of 1 lemon
- 6 Tbsp extra virgin olive oil
- 1 good pinch oregano
- 100g vine leaves
- 2 lemons, sliced finely
- freshly ground black pepper

1 Scale and gut the sardines, wash, remove heades and spines. Salt the fillets and place in a colander to drain.
2 Whisk the lemon juice with the extra virgin olive oil and oregano.
3 Preheat the oven to 200°C.
4 Oil a baking dish, line with a layer of vine leaves. Cover with half the sardines, pour on half the lemon-oil dressing, top with several slices of lemon. Then make another layer of vine leaves, sardines, lemon slices and a final layer of vine leaves. Cover the leaves with the remaining lemon slices and lemon-oil dressing.
5 Bake for about 30'.

SARDINE ROLLS

Sardhéles tilihtés

Serves 4 as a main course,

       8 as an appetiser or mezé with ouzo

- 1 kg very fresh sardines
- 700g ripe tomatoes, peeled, seeded, finely chopped and left to drain
- 1 large onion, finely chopped
- 1 bunch flat-leaf parsley, finely chopped
- salt to taste
- ½ cup extra virgin olive oil

1 Scale and gut the sardines, wash. Remove the head and spine, leaving about 1 cm [½ inch] at the end and the tail. Lay skin side down on a large tray. Continue with all the sardines.

2 Combine the tomatoes, onion, parsley and salt, and spread over the sardines with a spatula.

3 Roll up each sardine starting from the head end, with the vegetables on the inside, and use the remaining spine to spear the roll and keep it closed.

4 Arrange in a baking dish in neat rows with the tails pointing upwards. Pour on the extra virgin olive oil and bake on the bottom shelf of the oven at 200°C for about 20'-30' until done. Serve hot with a salad.

BAKED NEEDLEFISH WITH GARLIC

Zarghánes me skórdho sto fúrno

Serves 4

- 1½ kg medium garfish (needlefish)
- a little extra virgin olive oil
- 1 cup dry white wine
- 12 cloves garlic, puréed
- ½ cup flat-leaf parsley, finely chopped
- freshly ground black pepper
- salt

1 Preheat oven to 180°C.

2 Scale, gut and wash the fish. Season with salt and pepper and brush with a little extra virgin olive oil.

3 Bake in oven for 20'-25'. After the first 10' add the wine.

4 When the fish is done pull the heads downwards carefully and remove with the spine.

5 Combine the garlic purée with the finely chopped parsley and use this mixture to stuff the fish where the spine was.

Serve immediately.

GILT-HEADED SEA BREAM FILLETS WITH CELERY

Filéta tsipúras me sélino

Serves 4

- 4 gilt-headed sea bream (about 350g each)
- 1 kg tender dark celery leaves, coarsely chopped
- 1 cup extra virgin olive oil
- 4 spring onions [scallions], white parts only, finely sliced
- 2 carrots, scraped, sliced
- 2 juicy lemons
- 2 eggs, separated
- salt
- freshly ground black pepper

1 Scale, gut and remove the gills of the bream and wash well, being particularly careful to remove the bitter black membrane and blood in the belly cavity. Salt inside and out.

2 Trim and wash the celery leaves. Blanch for a few minutes in plenty of boiling water, drain and refresh with cold water.

3 Heat the extra virgin olive oil in a saucepan and sauté the onions lightly for 2'-3', add the carrots, celery, salt, pepper and the juice of 1 lemon, add enough water to barely cover, and simmer for 20'.

4 Grill [broil] the bream for 7'-8' on each side. Remove from heat. Using a sharp knife and starting from the head towards the tail carefully cut away the fillets.

5 Whisk the egg whites until stiff. Gradually add the yolks, the juice of the second lemon and 2 spoonfuls of the hot stock from the celery sauce.

6 Arrange the bream fillets on a serving platter, pour on the celery sauce, and top with the egg-lemon sauce.

COD CASSEROLE

Bakaliáros yahní

Serves 4

- 1 kg fresh cod
- 1 cup extra virgin olive oil
- 2 medium onions, finely diced
- 4 cloves garlic, peeled and lightly crushed
- 1 cup dry white wine
- 1 ripe tomato, peeled, seeded, finely chopped
- ½ cup flat-leaf parsley, finely chopped
- 1 Tbsp dill weed, finely chopped
- 4 medium potatoes, cut into pieces
- salt
- freshly ground black pepper

1 Scale, gut and remove the gills of the cod, wash and cut into portions. Season with salt and pepper.

2 Heat the extra virgin olive oil in a saucepan over a medium heat, and sear the fish for 1' on each side.

3 Add the onion and garlic, fry until translucent.

4 Add the wine, and when it stops sizzling, add the tomato, parsley, dill and potatoes. Cover the saucepan and simmer over a low heat for 20'-25'.

Serve hot.

BAKED FISH WITH HERBS

Psári sto fúrno me aromatiká hórta
Serves 4

- 1 bunch hartwort
- 1 bunch dill weed
- 4 leaves spearmint
- 4 leaves sage
- 4 spring onions [scallions]
- 500g spinach, leaves only
- 1.5 kg fish of your choice
- 1 cup extra virgin olive oil
- ½ cup dry white wine
- freshly ground black pepper & salt

For the sauce:
- freshly squeezed juice of one lemon
- 1 clove garlic, puréed
- ½ tsp mustard
- 1 cup extra virgin olive oil
- freshly ground black pepper & salt

1 Wash all the greens, herbs and spinach very well. Spin dry or leave to drain in a colander, then chop finely.

2 Preheat the oven to 200 °C.

3 Heat ½ cup extra virgin olive oil and stir-fry the greens for 5'-6'. Remove from the heat, season with salt and pepper and leave to cool

4 Scale, gut and remove the gills of the fish, wash, score the sides, remove head and spine.

5 Use the greens to stuff the fish and arrange in a baking dish.

6 Pour over the wine and ½ cup extra virgin olive and bake in the oven for 15'-20'.

7 Make the dressing by whisking the lemon juice, garlic, mustard, salt and pepper together very well, then gradually adding the second cup of extra virgin olive oil.

8 Pour the dressing over the fish and serve hot.

GRIDDLED PIKE

Lútsos sto mandémi
Serves 2

- 1 large, very fresh pike
- 1 cup extra virgin olive oil
- 2 cloves garlic, puréed
- 1 Tbsp oregano
- ½ cup flat-leaf parley, finely chopped
- freshly ground black pepper & salt

1 Scale, gut and remove the gills of the pike, and wash well. Season with salt and pepper and brush with a little extra virgin olive oil.

2 Preheat a cast-iron griddle.

3 Whisk together the extra virgin olive oil, garlic and oregano.

4 Oil the griddle, put the fish on it, and baste it frequently with the extra virgin olive oil mixture. Cook for 15'-20', turning over halfway through.

5 When done serve immediately, sprinkled with parsley.

cuttlefish with herbs

CUTTLEFISH WITH HERBS
Supiés me aromatiká hórta
Serves 4-6

- 1 kg cuttlefish, not very large
- 1 cup dry white wine
- 1 cup extra virgin olive oil
- 1 leek, finely
- 4 spring onions [scallions]
- ½ bunch each of fennel fronds, dill weed,
  hartwort
- 1 bunch dock
- 2 ripe tomatoes, peeled, seeded and finely diced
- freshly ground black pepper & salt

1 Prepare cuttlefish (see page 100), reserving one of the ink sacs. Wash thoroughly, turning inside out. Cut into pieces.

2 Squeeze a little of the ink from the reserved ink sac into the cup of wine.

3 Wash all the greens and herbs thoroughly. Spin dry or drain well in a colander. Chop finely.

4 Heat the extra virgin olive oil and sauté the leek and onion for 2'. Add the squid and stir-fry another 3'. Add the wine, cover the saucepan and cook over a medium heat for 30'.

5 Add the greens, herbs and tomato, 1 cup water, and season with salt and pepper. Cook over a low heat for 30'-35'. Uncover the pan towards the end of the cooking time if necessary to allow excess liquid to evaporate, so only the oil remains. Serve at room temperture.

RED MULLET EN PAPILLOTE
Barbúni sto hartí
(photo on page 151)
Serves 2

- 4 very fresh red mullet
- 3 Tbsp extra virgin olive oil
- 2 bay leaves
- ½ Tbsp rosemary or the leaves stripped off one
- 2 cloves garlic, finely sliced
- 2 slices lemon
- 1 sheet of greaseproof paper cut in half

1 Preheat the oven to 200 °C.

2 Scale and gut the red mullet, wash well, salt and leave to drain.

3 Place one bayleaf in the middle of each half sheet of paper, top with two fish, sprinkle each pair with half the rosemary, garlic and extra virgin olive oil, putting a little in the belly cavity as well, and top with one slice of lemon. Fold over the edges of the paper carefully to form a tight seal, but loosely around the fish to allow room for steam to build up inside.

4 Bake for about 20'.

5 Serve hot, cutting the paper open at the table to release the aroma.

BAKED TUNA WITH SAGE

Tónos me faskómilo sto fúrno

Serves 4

- 4 tuna steaks, 2-3cm thick
- 2 cups hot water
- 2 sprigs fresh sage
- 1 cup extra virgin olive oil
- 2 medium onions, finely diced
- 1 cup dry red wine
- ½ Tbsp butter, preferably from ewe's or goat's milk
- 2 potatoes, boiled, peeled and cut into 2cm thick slices
- salt
- freshly ground black pepper

1 Wash the tuna steaks thoroughly under running cold water to remove all the blood.

2 Bring the water to the boil, add the sage and strain after 3'.

3 Heat half the extra virgin olive oil and sauté the onion until translucent. Add the wine and slowly add the hot sage infusion while stirring constantly. Boil until the sauce thickens. Towards the end add the butter and season with salt and pepper.

4 Preheat the oven to broil.

5 Pour the remaining extra virgin olive oil over the bottom of a baking pan, arrange the tuna steaks on top and grill [broil] on one side for 10'.

6 Take the baking pan out of the oven, remove the tuna steaks and set aside. Arrange the potato slices in an even layer on the bottom, place the tuna steaks on top, cooked side down, and grill [broil] a further 8'.

7 Whisk the sauce and pour over.

Serve hot.

BOGUE WITH CAPERS

Ghópes me kápari

Serves 4

- 8 large bogue caught in the open sea
- a little extra virgin olive oil
- 1 cup capers, soaked in water to remove salt, drained
- 2 spring onions [scallions], finely sliced
- 4 Tbsp dill weed, finely chopped
- freshly squeezed juice of 1 small lemon
- salt
- freshly ground black pepper

1 Scale, gut and remove the gills of the bogue, and wash well.
Season with salt and pepper and brush with extra virgin olive oil.
2 Combine the caper, onion, dill and lemon juice.
Use this mixture to stuff the belly cavity of the fish.
3 Grill fish for 8'-10' on each side.
Serve immediately.

GARLIC PRAWNS [SHRIMP]

Gharídhes me skórdho

Serves 2

- 500g large prawns [shrimp]
- 4 Tbsp extra virgin olive oil
- 8 cloves garlic, finely sliced
- 1 fresh lemon, cut into wedges
- a pinch of coarse sea salt

1 Wash the prawns [shrimp]
2 Heat a large deep frying pan [skillet], add the oil,
prawns [shrimp], garlic and salt.
3 Fry the prawns [shrimp] on one side until golden, turn to the
other side, add the garlic cloves and fry for 2'.
4 Serve hot with lemon wedges.

bogue with capers

foods λαδερά cooked in oil

Ladherá

STUFFED COURGETTE [ZUCCHINI] FLOWERS

Kolokitholúludha yemistà

Serves 4

- 16 large courgette [zucchini] flowers
- 2 medium ripe tomatoes, peeled, seeded, finely chopped
  and left in a sieve to drain off the juices
- 200g rice
- 1 medium onion, finely chopped
- a little dill weed, finely chopped
- 2 leaves spearmint, finely chopped
- 1 cup extra virgin olive oil
- freshly ground black pepper
- salt

1 Wash the flowers very carefully so they do not break, leave to dry.

2 Combine the tomato flesh, rice, onion, dill weed, spearmint, half the oil, salt and pepper and mix together well.

3 Half-fill each courgette [zucchini] flower with the stuffing. Do not over-fill or they will burst as the rice expands when cooked. Fold the tips over to close and place in a layer in a saucepan. Add warm water to barely cover and the remaining oil, then simmer gently over a low heat for 25'-30'.

Serve at room temperature.

ARTICHOKES 'A LA POLITA' (IN THE STYLE OF CONSTANTINOPLE)

Aghináres 'ala políta'

Serves 6

- 8 fresh globe artichokes
- freshly squeezed juice of 2 + 1 lemons
- 2 Tbsp flour
- 1 cup extra virgin olive oil
- 2 onions, finely chopped
- 2 spring onions, finely chopped
- 3 carrots, sliced
- 4 medium potatoes, peeled and quartered
- salt
- freshly ground black pepper
- 2 cups hot water
- 2 Tbsp finely minced dill weed

1 Prepare the artichokes: leave on about 4-5cm of the stem, remove the outer leaves, cut in half, peel away all the hard parts, and remove the inner choke with a spoon. Leave in a basin with water and the juice of two of the lemons and the flour.

2 Heat the oil and sauté both types of onions until golden, add the carrots, potatoes, salt and pepper, juice of the third lemon, two cups of hot water and boil for 30' over a high heat.

3 Then lower the heat, add the artichokes and dill weed, and simmer until all the water has cooked away and only the oil remains.

Serve at room temperature.

AUBERGINE CASSEROLE

Melidzànes katsarólas

Serves 6

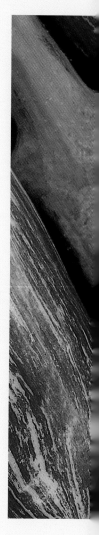

- 1 kg tender 'Slim Jim' aubergines [eggplants]
  (this is a long, thin, pointy variety, a reddish purple with pale lengthwise stripes)
- 1½ cups extra virgin olive oil
- 2 onions, finely chopped
- 4 cloves garlic, finely minced
- 1 kg very ripe tomatoes, peeled, seeded and finely chopped
- ½ tsp sugar
- salt
- freshly ground black pepper
- 350g green sweet peppers (capsicum) [bell peppers]
- 1 bunch flat-leaf parsley, leaves only
- 4-5 leaves spearmint

1 Drain the diced aubergines [eggplants] (see page 100).

2 Heat ½ cup of the extra virgin olive oil and sauté the onions with the garlic for 2'-3' until they brown lightly.

3 Add the tomato, sugar, salt and pepper and boil for 10'. Remove from heat and put sauce aside.

4 Wash the peppers, remove stems, seeds and inner pithy ribs, and cut in long strips.

5 Heat ½ cup extra virgin olive oil and stir-fry the aubergines [eggplants] and peppers for 3'. Remove and leave to drain.

6 Reheat the tomato sauce, then add the aubergines [eggplants] and peppers. Simmer, adding a little water if necessary.

After 30' add the remaining extra virgin olive oil, the spearmint and half the parsley. After 10' add the remaining parsley. Remove from heat and leave to cool.

Serve at room temperature with yoghurt or tzatziki.

Baked mixed vegetables

BAKED MIXED VEGETABLES

Briámi

Serves 8

• 4 'Slim Jim' aubergines [eggplants] (this is a
  long, thin, pointy variety, a reddish purple with
  pale lengthwise stripes)
• 4 courgettes [zucchini]
• 3 Hungarian wax peppers (called "horn" in
  Greek, a long pointy yellow-green sweet pepper
  (capsicum) [bell pepper], sliced finely
• 2 Florina peppers (a Greek variety, a fleshy,
  long pointy red sweet pepper (capsicum)
  [bell pepper])
• 3 medium potatoes, peeled
• 1 kg ripe tomatoes
• 2 medium onions, sliced
• 4 cloves garlic, finely minced
• 2 cups extra virgin olive oil
• 1 cup hot water
• 1 scant Tbsp sugar
• salt
• freshly ground black pepper
• ½ bunch flat-leaf parsley, finely chopped

1 Drain the sliced aubergines [eggplants]
(see page 100)
2 Preheat the oven to 200°C.
3 Wash and prepare the vegetables, cutting into
slices.
4 Layer all the vegetables except the parsley in a
baking pan, season with salt, pepper and sugar,
add the extra virgin olive oil and 1 cup hot water.
Cover and bake for about 60'.
5 Uncover, sprinkle with the parsley and bake for
another 15'.

6 Serve at room temperature, with feta cheese or
tzatziki.
The flavour improves if left standing for a few
hours.

POTATO-COURGETTE [ZUCCHINI] OMELETTE

Sfungáto

Serves 6

• 4 medium potatoes, boiled then peeled
• 3 medium courgettes [zucchini]
• 1 cup extra virgin olive oil
• 4 spring onions [scallions], white part only,
  finely sliced
• 1 onion, finely chopped
• 1 bunch dill weed, finely chopped
• salt
• freshly ground black pepper
• 8 eggs

1 Grate the boiled potatoes on the large holes of a
box grater and put aside.
2 Grate the raw courgettes [zucchini] on the large
holes of the grater, salt and leave in a large sieve
(or colander with small holes) to drain. Squeeze
between hands to remove excess juices.
3 Preheat the oven to 180°C.
4 Heat half the oil over a medium heat. Sauté the
onions until soft. Then add the grated courgettes
[zucchini] and stir-fry lightly until golden.
5 Remove with a slotted spoon and add to the
potatoes. Mix in the dill weed, spearmint, salt,
pepper and the well-beaten eggs.
6 Transfer to a small oiled baking dish, pour on
the remaining oil and bake until golden.
Serve at room temperature.

GREEN BEANS [FRENCH BEANS] WITH GARLIC

Fréska fasolákia me skórdho

Serves 6-8

- 750g green beans [French beans]
- ½ cup extra virgin olive oil
- 8 cloves garlic, sliced
- 1 Tbsp crushed zwieback or similar rusk
- 1 Tbsp flat-leaf parsley, finely chopped
- salt
- freshly ground black pepper

1 Wash the beans, snap off the tops and pull away any strings.

2 Bring a large saucepan full of water to a rolling boil over a high heat. Add the beans and boil for 8'-10'.

3 Remove from heat, drain and refresh by plunging immediately into cold water. Dry well.

4 Heat the oil over a low heat and add the remaining ingredients. Sauté lightly. Add the beans and stir-fry for 3'.

Serve at room temperature.

BAKED BUTTER BEANS

Yíghantes sto fúrno

Serves 8

- 500g dry butter beans [large lima beans]
- 1 cup extra virgin olive oil
- 2 leeks, washed carefully and sliced (white part only)
- 4 sun-dried tomatoes, finely chopped
- 1 kg ripe tomatoes, peeled, seeded and finely chopped
- 4 cloves garlic, finely sliced
- 3 Hungarian wax peppers (called "horn" in Greek), sliced finely
- 2 small hot chilli peppers, whole (optional)
- 2 carrots, scraped and sliced
- 1 Tbsp paprika
- 1 Tbsp tomato paste
- 1 scant Tbsp sugar
- freshly ground black pepper & salt
- ½ bunch flat-leaf parsley, finely chopped
- ½ bunch dill weed, finely chopped

1 Soak the beans in plenty of warm water for 12 hours, changing the water frequently (this reduces the beans' gaseous properties).

2 Bring 4 litres of water to the boil, add the beans, and boil rapidly for 10' counting from the moment the water returns to the boil. Do not salt the cooking water or the beans will toughen. Leave in this hot water for 2-3 hours. Drain and rinse.

3 Bring fresh water to the boil and add the beans. Boil over medium heat for about 1 hour until very soft. Drain, reserving the cooking liquid.

4 Preheat the oven to 200 °C.

5 Heat the oil in a deep frying pan [skillet] and sauté the leeks over a medium heat until soft. Then add all the remaining ingredients but only half the parsley and half the dill weed. Stir-fry lightly for 5', remove from heat.

6 Transfer the beans and the tomato sauce to an oiled baking dish with a cover. Add 2 cups of the reserved bean cooking liquid and mix lightly.

7 Bake on the bottom shelf of the oven, covered, at 200 °C for about 45'. Check the liquid from time to time and add more cooking liquid if necessary because the beans absorb a lot of moisure throughout their cooking time.

8 Remove the cover, sprinkle with the remaining parsley and dill weed, and transfer to the top shelf of the oven. Continue to bake for another 5'-10' until the beans brown slightly.

9 Do not serve immediately, but allow the beans to rest a while. Serve at room temperature, with feta cheese and taramosalata or tzatziki.

potatoes braised with oregano

POTATOES BRAISED WITH OREGANO

Patàtes righanàtes katsarólas

Serves 6

- 1 cup extra virgin olive oil
- 2 onions, finely chopped
- 1.5 kg potatoes, peeled and cut into pieces
- 2 cloves garlic, finely minced
- 2 tomatoes, peeled, seeded, finely chopped
- ½ Tbsp dried oregano
- salt
- freshly ground black pepper
- ½ Tbsp paprika
- ½ bunch flat-leaf parsley, finely chopped
- ½ Tbsp spearmint, finely chopped

1 Heat half the extra virgin olive oil over a medium heat and sauté the onion, stirring gently until translucent.

2 Add the potatoes, garlic, tomato, oregano, salt, pepper and paprika, the remaining extra virgin olive oil and enough hot water to barely cover the potatoes. Cook over a medium heat until the water evaporates and only the oil is left.

3 5' before the end of the cooking time add the parsley and spearmint.

Serve hot with feta cheese or kefalotiri.

MASHED POTATOES WITH EXTRA VIRGIN OLIVE OIL (PEASANT STYLE)

Patatopourés horiàtikos

Serves 4

- 5 medium potatoes
- 1 cup dry white wine
- salt
- freshly ground black pepper
- 1 cup extra virgin olive oil
- 1 tsp dry oregano
- 1 tsp dry thyme

1 Peel the potatoes and steam them until very soft, adding the wine to the boiling water.

2 Transfer to a large plate. Mash with a fork and season with salt and pepper.

3 Heat the oil in a large frying pan [skillet] over a high heat. Spread the mashed potatoes all over

the bottom and fry for about 10' until a crust is formed. Stir up with a wooden spatula and leave another 5' to form a crust again.

Serve hot or at room temperature, sprinkled with oregano and thyme.

NETTLE RISSOLES

Tsuknidhokeftédhes

Serves 10-12

- 1 kg tender nettle tips
- 3-4 slices stale bread, soaked in water, then squeezed well to remove excess water
- 1 cup flat-leaf parsley, finely chopped
- 1 Tbsp spearmint, finely chopped
- 2 eggs
- 2 cloves garlic, finely minced
- 1 Tbsp vinegar
- salt
- freshly ground black pepper
- 1 cup extra virgin olive oil
- a little additional extra virgin olive oil

1 Preheat the oven to 180 °C.

2 Wash the nettles carefully, wearing rubber gloves.

3 Bring water to the boil and blanch the nettles for 4'-5'. Drain and chop finely.

4 Combine all the ingredients well to make a smooth mass. Shape into patties.

5 Oil a baking tray, place the patties on it and roast until golden. Serve hot.

BAKED COURGETTES [ZUCCHINI]

Kolokithákia fúrnu

Serves 4

- 3 medium courgettes [zucchini]
- 8 Tbsp extra virgin olive oil
- 2-3 cloves garlic, finely sliced
- 200g strained yoghurt
- 2 cloves garlic, puréed
- a few spearmint leaves, finely chopped
- salt

1 Wash the courgettes [zucchini] and slice finely.

2 Oil a baking pan, spread out the courgette slices, sprinkle with salt and the sliced garlic, pour on the extra virgin olive oil.

3 Bake in the oven at 180 °C until golden, about 40'-50'.

4 In the meantime combine the yoghurt with the garlic purée and the spearmint in a small bowl.

5 Serve the courgettes [zucchini] hot with the yoghurt.

BAKED CHICK PEAS [GARBANZOS]

Revíthia fúrnu

Serves 8

- 500g dry chick peas [garbanzos] (be sure these are new season's)
- 2 onions, finely chopped
- 1 cup extra virgin olive oil
- 1 bunch dill weed, finely chopped
- 1 Tbsp rosemary
- 1 clove garlic, finely minced
- salt
- freshly ground black pepper
- ½-1 cup flour

1 Soak the chick peas [garbanzos] in plenty of warm water for 12 hours, changing the water frequently (this reduces the beans' gaseous properties).

2 Preheat the oven to 100 °C.

3 Bring plenty of water to the boil, add the chick peas [garbanzos], and boil rapidly for 10' counting from the moment the water returns to the boil. Drain, reserving 1-2 cups of the cooking liquor.

4 Combine all the ingredients except the flour in a lidded earthenware casserole or baking dish. Add enough hot cooking liquor to cover and put on the lid.

5 Make dough with flour and water and use it to seal the lid onto the baking dish.

6 Bake at 100 °C for 8 hours.

Serve at room temperature.

AMARANTH STEW

Vlíta yahní

Serves 4

- 1 kg amaranth greens, picked over (keep only the tender tips)
- ½ cup extra virgin olive oil
- 1 large onion, finely chopped
- 4 cloves garlic, finely minced
- 3 medium potatoes, peeled and cut into large cubes
- 1-2 cups hot water
- ½ tsp salt
- freshly ground black pepper

1 Wash the amaranth greens, drain and chop coarsely.

2 Heat the oil in a large saucepan over a medium heat and sauté the onion, garlic and potatoes until they begin to colour lightly, stirring from time to time.

3 Add the greens, salt and 1 cup hot water, stir and simmer, half-covered with the lid, over a low heat for 25'-35', adding more water if necessary, until the vegetables are very soft and all the water has evaporated, leaving only the oil.

4 Serve at room temperature with freshly ground black pepper.

hickpeas soaking in a clay baking dish in the courtyard
f a house on Sifnos (a traditional dish of this island)

ROAST POTATOES WITH ROSEMARY

Patátes fúrnu me dhendhrolívano

Serves 8

- 1.5 kg new [very small] potatoes, scrubbed well but not peeled
- 1 tsp paprika
- 4 cloves garlic, puréed
- ½ cup dry white wine
- salt
- freshly ground black pepper
- 2 + 1 tsp dry rosemary, or leaves stripped from 2-3 sprigs
- 1½ cups extra virgin olive oil
- freshly squeezed juice of 1 lemon
- 200g yoghurt
- ½ bunch spearmint, finely chopped

1 Preheat oven to 220 °C.

2 In a basin combine the potatoes, paprika, garlic, salt and pepper and 2 tsp rosemary.

3 Transfer to a baking pan. Pour on the extra virgin olive oil and stir.

4 Cover and roast at 220 °C for 20'-30' until the potatoes soften.

5 Uncover, stir, sprinkle with the remaining 1 tsp rosemary and roast another 20' until golden.

6 Add the lemon juice 5' before the end of the cooking time.

7 Combine the yoghurt with the spearmint.

8 Serve the potatoes at room temperature with the yoghurt.

BROAD BEANS WITH YOGHURT

Kukiá me yaúrti

Serves 6

- 1 kg tender broad beans (use very young beans with edible pods)
- 1 cup extra virgin olive oil
- 2 onions, finely chopped
- ½ bunch dill weed or fennel fronds, finely chopped
- ½ bunch flat-leaf parsley, finely chopped
- 2 Tbsp spearmint, finely chopped
- 2 cups hot water
- salt
- freshly ground black pepper
- 200g yoghurt
- 2 cloves garlic, puréed

1 Wash the broad beans [fava beans], dry, snap off the top and pull down, then snap in half, removing any strings that may appear.

2 Heat the extra virgin olive oil and sauté the onion until translucent.

3 Add the broad beans [fava beans], dill or fennel, parsley, spearmint, and 2 cups hot water. Stir gently, then simmer over low heat until soft, adding more water if necessary. Do not stir once soft or the pods will open, shake the pan gently from side to side instead. Cook until all the water evaporates and only the oil remains.

4 Combine the yoghurt with the garlic.

5 Serve at room temperature or cold, with the yoghurt on the side.

pasta, rice

Zimariká, rízi

short macaroni with her

SHORT MACARONI WITH HERBS

Makaronáki koftó me mirodhiká

Serves 4-6

- 500g short macaroni such as tubetti or ditali
- I cup extra virgin olive oil
- 3 cloves garlic, finely minced
- I cup flat-leaf parsley, finely chopped
- ½ cup fresh basil leaves, finely chopped
- ½ cup fresh spearmint leaves, finely chopped
- ½ cup fresh dill fronds, finely chopped
- I tsp sage, finely chopped
- I tsp oregano, finely chopped
- I tsp thyme, finely chopped
- I tsp rosemary, finely chopped
- I small hot chilli pepper (optional)
- salt
- freshly ground black pepper
- freshly ground cheese (optional)

I Bring plenty of water to a rolling boil, add I tsp salt and the macaroni, stir. Boil al dente, drain and reserve I cup of the cooking water.

2 Heat the oil over a low heat and add the garlic. When golden add all the herbs. Stir-fry lightly, stirring with a wooden spoon, until the herbs release their aroma, about 5'. Season with salt and pepper.

3 Combine the herb mixture with the macaroni and the reserved cooking water, toss well.

4 Serve hot, with freshly grated cheese (optional).

RISOTTO WITH LEEKS, DILL AND LEMON

Rizótto me prása, ánitho ke lemóni

Serves 4

- 2 cups leeks, finely sliced
- 5 Tbsp extra virgin olive oil
- I½ cups short-grain rice
- 5 cups hot vegetable stock
- ½ cup dill weed, finely chopped
- salt
- freshly ground black pepper
- ½ lemon, the zest and the juice
- I cup ghraviéra (a kind of gruyere cheese), grated

I Heat 3 Tbsp extra virgin olive oil in a wide saucepan over medium heat and sauté the leek until soft. Remove from the pan and set aside.

2 Heat 2 more Tbsp extra virgin olive oil in the pan and add the rice, stir for 2'.

3 Carefully pour in I cup of the hot vegetable stock (it will sizzle) and stir with a wooden spoon until all the liquid is absorbed. Immediately add a second cup of stock, and repeat the procedure until you add the last cupful of stock. Then stir in the leek and the dill weed and continue stirring until the liquid is nearly all absorbed: the rice should be creamy but not watery.

4 Just before the end of the cooking time stir in the seasonings: salt and pepper, lemon juice and zest, and the grated cheese.

Serve immediately.

risotto with leeks, dill weed and lemon

fisherman's rice

Wash thoroughly. Wash the prawns and Dublin Bay prawns.

2 Bring the water to a boil, add the seafood. Boil for 3'-4', remove from heat, keep aside the seafood, strain the cooking liquor and reserve.

3 Heat the olive oil and sauté the onion and bell pepper over a medium heat. Then add the seafood and black pepper, stir lightly for 2'-3', add the ouzo.

4 Add the reserved cooking liquor, turn up the heat and when it comes to a boil add the salt, rice and lemon juice. Cook for about 15' until the liquid is absorbed.

Serve immediately.

FISHERMAN'S RICE

Rízi tu psarà

Serves 4

- 8 large mussels with shell
- 4 large fresh prawns [shrimp]
- 4 large fresh Dublin Bay prawns [langoustines]
- 6 cups water
- ½ cup extra virgin olive oil
- 2 medium onions, finely chopped
- 1 green or red pepper (capsicum) [bell pepper], sliced
- 2 Tbsp ouzo
- freshly ground black pepper
- 1 ½ cups rice
- salt
- freshly squeezed juice of 1 lemon

1 Scrub the mussel shells and pull away the beard.

ARTICHOKE RICE

Anginarórizo

Serves 4

- 8 artichokes
- ½ cup extra virgin olive oil
- 1 onion, finely diced
- 2 spring onions [scallions], finely sliced
- 1 + 5 cups hot water
- 500g short-grain rice (for pilaf)
- salt
- freshly ground black pepper
- the freshly squeezed juice of 1 + 1 lemons (reserve the lemon cups)

egg noodles with aubergines

1 Pull away the hard outer leaves of the artichoke, cut in half and remove the hairy choke with a knife or spoon. Rub exposed areas with the inside of the lemon cups as you are working. Finely slice the tender hearts and quickly drop into water with lemon juice so they do not blacken.

2 Heat the extra virgin olive oil in a saucepan, add the onions and drained artichokes and sauté lightly. Add 1 cup water, turn down the heat and simmer for 10'.

3 Add the remaining 5 cups water, turn up the heat and as soon as it comes to a rolling boil add the rice and salt, stir, turn down the heat to low and simmer until the liquid is absorbed.

4 Add pepper, lemon juice and serve hot.

EGG NOODLES WITH AUBERGINES [EGGPLANTS]

Hilopíttes me melidzánes

Serves 6

- 1 kg aubergines [eggplant]
- ½ cup extra virgin olive oil
- 2 cloves garlic, finely minced
- 4 tomatoes, peeled, seeded and puréed
- salt
- freshly ground black pepper
- 500g egg noodles, fettuccine or tagliatelle
- 1 cup grated cheese

1 Wash the aubergines [eggplant], remove the stems, cut in halves, salt and leave in a colander to drain for 30'.

2 Heat the extra virgin olive oil in a deep frying pan [skillet], add the garlic, tomato, salt and pepper and sauté for about 10' over a medium heat.

3 Rinse the aubergines [eggplant] and cut into strips lengthwise. Add to the tomato mixture, turn the heat down and simmer for about 40' until excess liquid boils away from the sauce and only the oil remains.

4 Bring salted water to a rolling boil, add the egg noodles and boil for 5'-8' until tender. Strain, retaining a little of the cooking water.

5 Add the sauce, a little cooking water, and the grated cheese. Mix lightly and serve immediately.

FRESH HOMEMADE PASTA WITH VEGETABLE SAUCE

Fréska hiropíyta makarónia me sàltsa lahanikón

Serves 6

For the pasta
- 2½ + 1 cups hard flour
- ½ tsp salt
- 3 eggs

For the sauce
- 1 cup extra virgin olive oil
- 1 medium onion, finely chopped
- 1 medium courgette [zucchini], finely diced
- 1 aubergine [eggplant], diced and degorged
- 1 red sweet pepper, seeded and cut in fine strips
- 1 cup ripe tomatoes, peeled, seeded, finely diced
- ½ cup fresh basil or spearmint leaves, finely chopped
- salt
- freshly ground black pepper
- ½ cup black olives, pitted
- 80g mizithra (a hard white cheese, very salty), freshly grated

1 To make the pasta, sift 2½ cups flour with the salt onto a large flat surface. Mound it and make a well in the middle. Beat the eggs well and pour into the well. Draw flour in from the sides towards the middle until mixed with the egg. Sprinkle flour on top and knead for 10' until a smooth elastic dough is formed. Sprinkle with more flour if needed. Form into a ball, cover with a clean kitchen towel and leave to rest for 20'.

2 Knead again for 5' to become very pliable, cover again and leave to rest another 20'.

3 Roll small pieces of dough between your palms to form thick 'sausages' about 5cm long, then pinch the ends together with your fingers to form a ring. Place on a lightly floured surface and leave to dry for 15'.

4 To make the sauce, heat the extra virgin olive oil and sauté the onion over a low heat until translucent. Add the remaining ingredients except the olives and cheese and cook until soft.

5 Bring plenty of water to a rolling boil, add 1 tsp salt and the pasta, stir and boil for 6'-8'. Do not allow to become soggy. Drain and tip into the vegetable sauce, stirring to coat well.

6 Place on a serving platter. Sprinkle with cheese and olives and serve hot.

STUFFED CABBAGE ROLLS

Yaprákia me láhano

Serves 8

- 1 medium cabbage
- ½ cup extra virgin olive oil
- 1 onion, finely chopped
- 1 large leek, finely sliced
- salt
- freshly ground black pepper
- ½ tsp ground cumin
- 1 tsp paprika
- 2 cups hot water
- 250g rice
- freshly squeezed juice of 1 lemon
- 1 cup dill weed, finely chopped

1 Cut out the hard core of the cabbage with a pointed knife. Immerse the cabbage in a large pan of boiling salted water. Using tongs or long-handled spoons peel off the outer layers of leaves as they soften, and plunge in cold water to refresh. Drain.

2 Heat the oil in a frying pan [skillet] and sauté the onion and leek until they brown slightly. Add the seasonings, rice, lemon juice and a little water. Stir lightly for 2'-3' minutes until well mixed, remove from heat.

3 Cut out the thick rib running up the centre of each cabbage leaf, reserve. Overlap the cut edges of each leaf, place 2 Tbsp of filling in a line across, then roll up into a long cigar shape, making sure all the edges are folded over so the filling cannot escape.

4 Line the bottom of a heavy saucepan with the reserved cabbage leaf ribs. Carefully layer the cabbage rolls on top of the ribs. Add enough hot water to barely cover them and cook over a low heat for about 35'.

5 Serve at room temperature sprinkled with finely chopped dill weed

EGG NOODLES WITH MUSHROOMS

Hilopíttes me manitária

Serves 4

- 400g fresh champignon mushrooms
- 500g egg noodles, fettuccine or tagliatelle
- 1 + 4 Tbsp extra virgin olive oil
- 4 cloves garlic, finely sliced
- 1 cup kefalotiri (a hard salty cheese), grated
- 1 bunch flat-leaf parsley, leaves only, finely chopped
- freshly ground black pepper
- salt

1 Brush the mushrooms gently to remove any dirt, rinse quickly under running water, drain and dry. Slice finely.

2 Bring plenty of water to a rolling boil, add 1 tsp salt and the noodles, stir. Boil for about 8' or until still al dente. Drain and add 1 Tbsp extra virgin olive oil, mix and keep warm.

3 Heat 4 Tbsp extra virgin olive oil in a frying pan [skillet], add the mushrooms and the garlic and stir-fry until the juices have evaporated and they have turned golden brown.

4 Put the noodles on a large serving platter. Add the mushrooms and toss well. Sprinkle with the cheese, parsley and pepper.

Serve hot.

WILD ASPARAGUS WITH PASTA

Agria sparangi me zimarika

Serves 4

- 400g wild asparagus
- 500g pasta of choice
- 1 cup extra virgin olive oil
- 4 cloves garlic, finely sliced
- 2 shallots, finely chopped
- 1 cup extra virgin olive oil
- freshly ground black pepper
- salt

1 Bring 2 litres of water to a roiling boil, add 1 tsp salt and the washed asparagus. Boil for only 1-2' until still al dente and remove from the water with tongs or with a slotted spoon.

2 Place the pasta in the boiling water and cook until al dente.

3 In a frying pan [skillet] heat the olive oil and saute the shallots and garlic until transluscent. Add the asparagus, saute for 1' and remove from the heat.

4 Pour the sauce over the pasta, gind black pepper on top and serve immediately.

BAKED ORZO

Kritharáki fúrnu

Serves 6

- 400g orzo (pasta shaped like very large grains of rice)
- 6 Tbsp extra virgin olive oil
- 2 cups tomatoes, peeled, seeded and finely chopped
- 1 medium onion, finely diced
- 3 Hungarian wax peppers (called "horn" in Greek, a long pointy yellow-green sweet pepper (capsicum) [bell pepper]), sliced finely
- 1 small hot chilli pepper (optional)
- 1 stalk celery with leaves, finely chopped
- 3 cloves garlic, finely sliced
- ½ cup dill weed, finely chopped
- 2 cups vegetable stock
- salt
- freshly ground black pepper
- 140g ghraviéra cheese (Greek gruyere), coarsely grated

1 Bring plenty of water to a rolling boil, add 1 tsp salt and the orzo, stir. Boil for 6' or until still al dente, drain and reserve 2 cups of the cooking water.

2 Place in a lightly oiled baking pan, add the reserved water and all the remaining ingredients except the cheese.

3 Bake at 230 °C for about 15' or until it has absorbed nearly all of the cooking liquid. It may still be a little moist because it will continue to swell and absorb the liquid after coming out of the oven.

4 Sprinkle with the cheese and serve at room temperature.

SPAGHETTI WITH DUBLIN BAY PRAWNS [LANGOUSTINES]

Karavídhes me makarónia

Serves 6

- 1 kg Dublin Bay prawns [langoustines]
- ½ cup extra virgin olive oil
- 4 cloves garlic, finely minced
- 3 large ripe tomatoes, peeled, seeded, finely chopped
- ½ cup dry white wine
- 1 bunch flat-leaf parsley, finely chopped
- 500g spaghetti
- salt
- lots of freshly ground black pepper

1 Bring a pot of water to a rolling boil and cook the Dublin Bay prawns [langoustines] for 4'. Drain, reserving the cooking liquor, and allow to cool slightly. Then discard the heads, use scissors to cut each side of the undershell, and peel back the shell to remove the meat. Set aside. Strain the reserved stock through a very fine sieve and return to the rinsed pot.

2 Heat the extra virgin olive oil in a deep frying pan [skillet] and sauté the garlic lightly for 2'-3'. Add the tomatoes, season with salt and pepper and simmer over low heat for 5'-7'.

3 Add the prawn meat, wine, parley and lots of freshly ground black pepper and continue to simmer until the sauce thickens.

4 Bring the prawn stock to a rolling boil and add the spaghetti. Stir and cook until al dente. Drain.

5 Pour the sauce over the spaghetti, grind more black pepper on top and serve immediately.

spaghetti with dublin bay prawns [langoustines

desserts, cakes

Ghliká

range preserve / orange spoon sweet

ORANGE PRESERVE

Portokáli ghlikó

Serves 10-12

- 4 large, thick-skinned oranges
- 3½ cups water
- 1 kg sugar
- 1 Tbsp lemon juice

1 Wash the oranges well and grate all over to remove the zest. (This can be kept in an airtight container in the freezer for use elsewhere.)

2 Put the oranges in a saucepan, cover with cold water, bring to the boil and simmer for 15'. Drain and leave to cool.

3 Repeat the previous step with fresh water, simmering another 15'. Drain and leave to cool.

4 Cut the oranges downwards into quarters, then each quarter in half across, resulting in eight pieces from each orange. Cut away the tough edges of the inner membranes with scissors.

5 In a large saucepan heat the water with the sugar, stirring until dissolved. Add the orange pieces and boil furiously without a lid for 30'. Remove from heat, cover and leave for 24 hours.

6 The following day stir in the lemon juice and bring to the boil again, boiling furiously until the syrup thickens, because the oranges will have released their juices overnight.

7 Store the orange pieces covered with the syrup in an airtight jar.

FLUTES

Floyéres

About 25 pieces

- 1 cup walnuts, coarsely chopped
- 1 cup almonds, coarsely chopped
- 2 Tbsp crushed zwieback or similar rusk
- 1 tsp ground cinnamon
- 1 tsp ground cloves
- 2 Tbsp sugar
- 500g phyllo pastry
- 1 cup light extra virgin olive oil
- 1 cup powdered sugar

1 Preheat the oven to 180 °C.

2 Combine the nuts, zwieback, spices and sugar.

3 Cut the sheets of phyllo pastry in half.

4 Brush each half-sheet with extra virgin olive oil, fold in half, brush again with oil. Place one Tbsp of nut mixture lengthways down the middle and wrap up in the shape of a flute or cigar.

5 Oil a baking tray and arrange the flutes on it. Bake in the preheated oven at 180 °C for 20'-30' until lightly golden.

6 Dust with powdered sugar.

flute

CRETAN PIES STUFFED WITH WHITE CHEESE

Kaltsúnia kritiká me anthótiro

About 25-30 pieces

For the dough:
- 1Kg soft flour
- 25g fresh yeast or 1 packet instant dry yeast
- warm water
- 1 cup extra virgin olive oil
- 250g sugar
- 3 eggs, lightly beaten
- ½ tsp salt
- 3 Tbsp strained yoghurt

For the filling:
- 800g anthótiro (fresh unsalted soft white cheese, or substitute cottage cheese or ricotta)
- 1 egg yolk
- 1 tsp vanilla essence
- 2 Tbsp thyme honey
- 1 tsp lemon zest
- ½ tsp ground cinnamon
- 1 tsp butter
- 150g powdereded sugar
- 1 egg yolk, diluted with a little water
- a little extra virgin olive oil

1 Preheat the oven to 180 °C.

2 In a large basin dissolve the fresh yeast in warm water, add a handful of the flour, knead well and leave in a warm place to rise. (This step can be skipped when using instant dry yeast; simply mix it into the flour and go on to the next step.

3 Beat the extra virgin olive oil with the sugar. Add the eggs, salt, yoghurt and the yeast mixture (or the warm water if using instant dry yeast) and mix well. Add the remaining flour and knead. Leave the dough to rise in a warm place while preparing the filling.

4 Combine the white cheese, egg yolk, vanilla, honey, zest, cinnamon and butter. Gradually add the sugar and mix well.

5 Roll out the dough to a medium thickness and cut it into rounds.

6 Put a teaspoonful of the filling in the centre of each round and seal the dough into a half-moon shape by pinching it all around. Brush with diluted yolk.

7 Place on an oiled tray and bake in the oven at 180 °C for about 30'.

YOGHURT CAKE

Yaurtópita

About 18 pieces

- 3 Tbsp butter made of ewe's or goat's milk, melted
- 2½ cups sugar
- 300g natural yoghurt (not strained)
- 6 eggs, separated
- zest of 1 lemon
- zest and juice of 1 orange
- 1 cup blanched almonds, coarsely chopped
- 2 tsp vanilla essence
- a little extra butter
- a little extra flour

1 Preheat oven to 180 °C.

2 Beat the butter with the sugar for about 10' until fluffy.

3 Gradually add the egg yolks, the citrus zests and juice, almonds, vanilla and flour, mixing until smooth.

4 Whisk the egg whites until stiff and gently fold in.

5 Butter a baking pan, dust lightly with flour, and pour in the mixture.

6 Bake at 180 °C for 10', then lower to 160 °C and bake a further 50'-60'.

BAKED QUINCE WITH YOGHURT

Kidhónia sto fúrno me yaúrti

Serves 8

- 4 large quinces
- 6 leaves of scented-leaf geranium (Pelargonium quercifolium P. crispum)
- 8 Tbsp dark brown sugar
- 8 cloves
- 1 cup blanched almonds, coarsely chopped
- 400g strained yoghurt
- 8 Tbsp white sugar
- 2 tsps honey
- a little extra virgin olive oil

1 Wash the quinces thoroughly, rubbing to remove the down, cut in half, peel and core. Place in a saucepan, add enough water to barely cover, add the scented geranium leaves and simmer for 15'. Drain and reserve the cooking liquid.

2 Arrange the quince halves in a baking pan, cut side up, and fill each hollow where the seeds were with 1 Tbsp dark brown sugar. Sprinkle all over with the white sugar and pour the strained cooking liquid into the baking pan.

3 Bake, covered, for 30' at 200 °C. Uncover, press a clove into each piece and bake, uncovered, another 30' until they turn a warm pink colour.

4 Gently remove the quince halves from the baking pan onto individual dessert plates. Pour the cooking liquid into a small saucepan and boil over a low heat until it thickens, adding the honey towards the end.

5 Heat a heavy, lightly oiled frying pan [skillet] over medium heat, then turn the heat down to low and toast the almonds until golden, stirring frequently to make sure they do not burn. Drain on paper towels.

6 Serve each quince half with a dollop (2Tbsp) of yoghurt, pour on a little hot syrup and sprinkle with the freshly toasted almonds.

SEMOLINA CAKE

Sámali

About 24 pieces

For the cake:
- 3½ cups coarse semolina
- 3 cups sugar
- 3 tsp baking powder
- 1½ cups milk
- zest of 1 lemon
- zest of 1 orange
- a little extra virgin olive oil
- a little flour

For the syrup:
- 4 cups water
- 1½ cups sugar
- ½ orange
- ½ cup honey

1 Combine all the cake ingredients and mix well.

2 Preheat the oven to 140 °C.

3 Oil a baking pan, dust lightly with flour. Pour in the cake mixture and leave to rest for 30'.

4 Bake at 140 °C for about 60' until golden and a crust forms. Remove from oven and leave to cool.

5 Prepare the syrup by boiling the water, sugar and orange together until it thickens. Towards the end remove the orange and add the honey, stirring well.

6 Pour the warm syrup over the cold cake in the baking pan. Leave until the syrup is absorbed, then cut the cake while still in the pan.

SPICY BISCUITS [COOKIES] WITH EXTRA VIRGIN OLIVE OIL

Aromatiká kulurákia me eleóladho

About 30 pieces

- 1-2 cups sugar (depending on desired sweetness)
- 2 cups extra virgin olive oil
- 1 cup orange juice
- the zest of one orange
- ½ cup brandy
- ½ cup ouzo
- 1 tsp baking soda
- 1 tsp baking powder
- 2 tsp ground cinnamon
- 1 tsp ground cloves
- 1 kg soft flour
- ½ tsp salt
- sesame seeds

1 Preheat oven to 180 °C.

2 Mix all the ingredients except the sesame very well until smooth.

3 Form the dough into whatever shapes you like (small rings are traditional, hence the Greek name) and coat all over with sesame seeds.

4 Bake for about 30' until golden.

CARROT CAKE WITH EXTRA VIRGIN OLIVE OIL
Kéik me caróto ke eleóladho

About 18 pieces

- 6 eggs
- 2 cups sugar
- 2 cups grated carrot
- zest of 2 oranges
- 1/4 cup Yellow Grand Marnier or Cointreau
- 2½ cups self-raising flour
- 1 cup extra virgin olive oil
- a little extra virgin olive oil
- a little additional flour

1 Preheat the oven to 160 °C.

2 Cream the eggs with the sugar until fluffy.

3 Add the carrot, zest and liqueur. Then gradually add the flour and extra virgin olive oil, mixing well.

4 Oil a baking dish and dust lightly with flour. Pour in the mixture.

5 Bake in the preheated oven at 160°C for 50'-55'.

TAHINI PUDDING
Halvás me tahíni

About 18 pieces

- 1½ cups sesame oil
- 4 cups flour
- 400g tahini
- 1 cup honey
- ½ cup almonds, coarsely chopped
- a little butter

1 Heat the sesame oil in a heavy-bottomed saucepan over a low heat. Add the flour and keep stirring until it turns a dark colour. Add the tahini and mix well.

2 Warm the honey and add to the mixture, then stir in the almonds.

3 Spread the mixture while hot on a buttered marble slab and form into a square or rectangle 2 cm [1 inch] thick. Cut into squares with a wet knife before it cools completely.

CHRISTMAS SHORTBREADS WITH EXTRA VIRGIN OLIVE OIL
Kurabiédhes me eleóladho

About 36 pieces

- 500g blanched almonds
- 2 cups extra virgin olive oil
- ½ cup sugar
- 2 tsp ouzo
- 2 tsp vanilla essence
- 1 tsp baking soda
- 1 Tbsp lemon juice
- 1 kg soft flour
- 500g powdered sugar.

1 Preheat the oven to 200 °C and toast the almonds until golden, watching that they do not burn.

2 Beat the extra virgin olive oil with the sugar until it whitens, preferably using a mixer. Then add the ouzo, vanilla and the baking soda dissolved in the lemon juice. Gradually add the flour until the dough is rather firm and does not stick to the fingers.

3 Form into any shape you like (a crescent moon shape is traditional) burying one or two almonds in each.

4 Place some distance apart on a lightly oiled baking tray and bake at 200 °C for 15', then at 150 °C for 5'-10' until golden.

5 Remove and while still hot dust thickly all over with powdered sugar.

carrot cake with extra virgin olive oil

RICE CAKE

Ravaní me rízi

About 18 pieces

- 1½ cups extra virgin olive oil
- 200g almonds, blanched and coarsely chopped
- 10 cups hot water
- 1 kg sugar
- 5 cups short-grain rice
- 1 level tsp ground cinnamon
- ½ scant tsp ground cloves
- a little additional ground cinnamon

1 Preheat oven to 200 °C.

2 Heat the extra virgin olive oil over a medium heat in a large saucepan and stir in the almonds until golden, watching that they do not burn.

3 Gradually add the hot water and the sugar, stirring constantly, then the rice, cinnamon and cloves. Continue stirring until the mixture thickens and comes away from the sides of the pan.

4 Oil a baking dish and dust lightly with flour. Pour the rice mixture into it and spread to cover.

5 Bake in the oven at 200 °C for 15', then turn the oven down to 160 °C and bake a further 45' or until golden

6 Serve with a sprinkling of ground cinnamon.

WALNUT CAKE WITH EXTRA VIRGIN OLIVE OIL

Karidhópitta me eleóladho

About 18 pieces

- 1 cup sugar
- 4 eggs
- 1 cup extra virgin olive oil
- 100g wholemeal flour
- 400g self-raising flour
- 1 tsp baking soda
- zest and juice of 1 lemon
- zest and juice of 2 oranges
- ¼ cup brandy
- 1 Tbsp mixed spice
- 200g walnuts, coarsely chopped
- 1 cup currants
- a little extra virgin olive oil
- a little flour

1 Preheat the oven to 180 °C.

2 Cream the sugar with the eggs, then gradually add the oil, flours, and baking soda and mix well. Add the citrus zests and juices, the brandy, spice, nuts and currants and mix well.

3 Oil a baking dish and dust lightly with flour. Pour in the mixture.

4 Bake in the preheated oven at 180 °C for 50'-60'.

TAHINI CAKE

Kéik me tahíni

About 18 pieces

- 2½ cups tahini, diluted in 1 cup warm water
- freshly squeezed juice of 1 orange
- 1 tsp baking soda
- 3 Tbsp dark rum
- 1 cup sugar
- 2 cups self-raising flour
- ½ cup walnuts, coarsely chopped
- ½ cup currants
- ½ cup sesame seeds, toasted
- zest of 1 orange
- 1 Tbsp mixed spice
- 2 tsp baking powder
- 2 Tbsp extra virgin olive oil

- 1 cup powdered sugar

1 Preheat the oven to 180 °C.

2 Mix well the diluted tahini, orange juice, the baking soda dissolved in the rum, and the sugar.

3 In another basin combine the flour, walnuts, currants, sesame, zest, spices and baking powder. Add to the tahini mixture and mix well.

4 Thoroughly oil a baking dish and pour in the mixture.

5 Bake in the preheated oven at 180 °C for 40'-50', testing with a skewer to see whether it is done.

6 Allow to cool slightly. Turn out of the baking dish and dust with powdered sugar.

ALMOND SWEETMEATS
Amighdhalotá
About 38 small pieces

almond sweetmeats

- 1+1 cups powdered sugar
- 2 cups water
- 3 cups ground blanched almonds
  (grind to a fine meal in food processor)
- 1 Tbsp fine semolina
- 4 egg whites
- 1 tsp vanilla essence
- 1 Tbsp freshly squeezed lemon juice
- rosewater or orange blossom water
- ½ cup whole blanched almonds
- additional powdered sugar

1 Preheat the oven to 180 °C.

2 Make a syrup by boiling 1 cup of powdered sugar with 2 cups of water over a medium heat. Allow to cool.

3 Combine syrup with the ground almonds and the semolina in a basin.

4 Whisk the egg whites until stiff, add the vanilla and lemon juice and mix gently into the other ingredients in the basin to form a soft dough that does not stick to the sides of the basin (add water if necessary). Leave to rest 15'.

5 Dampen hands with flower water and form small pear-shaped balls of dough. Bury one whole blanched almond in each.

6 Line a baking tray with greaseproof paper. Place the almond sweetmeats on this, leaving some space between each one. Bake for about 10' until a light golden colour, watching that they do not burn.

7 Allow to cool slightly, sprinkle with flower water and dust generously with powdered sugar.

Vegetarianism and its limits

Many vegetarians have chosen a meatless regime because they want to avoid the chronic diseases associated with overconsumption of meat and other animal flesh foods. The fibre and nutrients in fruits and vegetables have been proven to fight chronic deiseases and reduce mortality rates. But strict vegetarians (especially vegans and macrobiotics) risk a higher deficiency of essential nutrients such as proteins, B complex vitamins, calcium and trace minerals. Vegetarians must understand the basic principles of nutrition to ensure their good health.

Complete proteins are found only in foods of animal origin: meat, poultry, fish and seafood, dairy products and eggs. However, with a little care it is possible to meet the body's protein needs from plant sources by increasing consumption of fruits and vegetables, nuts (particularly raw almonds) and pulses [legumes], eating a large variety of foods, and combining incomplete proteins from complementary sources to form complete proteins (such as grains with pulses or nuts/seeds), or by adding a little milk or cheese.

Vitamin B12 is mainly found in foods of animal origin. Alternative sources are soy products and supplements. Soya beans and cereals also meet part of the need for Vitamin D, while exposure to sunlight (so abundant in Greece!) helps the body to produce this vitamin. Calcium is found in large quantities mainly in dairy products such as milk, yoghurt and cheese. This mineral is essential for developing bones and protecting them from the brittleness caused by age (osteoporosis). Meeting calcium needs without dairy products requires supplements or enriched juices and soy milk. Other sources of calcium are some pulses [legumes], dark green vegetables, such as broccoli, and raw nuts.

Iron can be added to the daily diet by pulses [legumes], leafy green vegetables, wholemeal bread and enriched cereals. Soluble iron in foods of plant origin is much lower than that found in red meat and other animal flesh foods. However, if the meal is rich in Vitamin C, this significantly increases the amount of iron that can be absorbed. Zinc is also an essential mineral. Good plant sources include pulses [legumes], leafy green vegetables, wholemeal bread, cereals and soy products.

The key to a healthy vegetarian diet is a balance in choosing the right foods to eat daily, such as fruits, vegetables, pasta, bread, cereals, rice, pulses [legumes], nuts or seeds and extra virgin olive oil, rather than excluding particular foods. Bon appétit!

translator's note

It is a challenge to render the pronunciation of one language with the letters of another language, particularly when certain phonemes (sounds) that exist in one have no exact correspondence in the other. The situation is complicated in Greek, where the pronunciation (as that of every other language) has changed over the centuries, but the orthography of the Ancient Greek language is already familiar to the English-speaking reader through the many words borrowed from Ancient Greek. Furthermore, there is debate as to how these sounds were pronounced.

A compromise has been found for this book: Ancient Greek words follow the established conventions of transliteration, making their etymological connexion with English and Latin more evident. Modern Greek words, however, are rendered phonetically, as they are pronounced today. This means that the orthographic continuity between many Ancient and Modern Greek words is lost, which may disappoint readers of a linguistic bent who wish to trace the etymology of the modern language, but will aid readers visiting Greece or resident here who wish to purchase the foods, order them in a restaurant or discuss them with their Greek friends.

Modern Greek words are rendered thus:

Vowels are pronounced as in Italian or Spanish:

a	as in arm
e	as in bed (rendered e, ai, ae in Ancient Greek transliteration)
i	between sit and seat (rendered i, e, ai, ei, oi, oe, y in Ancient Greek transliteration)
o	as in hot
u	between put and foot (rendered ou or u in Ancient Greek transliteration)

Most consonants are as in English. Some details:

th	as in think (rendered th in Ancient Greek transliteration)
dh	as in that (rendered d in Ancient Greek transliteration)
gi	hard as in give
ge	hard as in get
f	(rendered ph, u [as in au, eu] in Ancient Greek transliteration)
v	(rendered b, u [as in au, eu] in Ancient Greek transliteration)

Some consonants do not exist in English:

h	has a throatier quality, like the Scottish loch, before a, o, u, and is almost a hiss, like the German ich, before e and i (rendered ch in Ancient Greek transliteration)
gh	a soft sound far back in the throat, as though gargling (rendered g in Ancient Greek transliteration)

index of edible greens

index of recipes

bibliography

Γεννάδιος Π., *Λεξικόν Φυτολογικόν,* Αθήναιος, *Δειπνοσοφισταί,* Κάκτος, Αθήνα 1998
Θεόφραστος, *Φυτολογικό Λεξικό κατά Θεόφραστο,* Σύνταξη Ρένα Καρακατσάνη, Κάκτος, Αθήνα 1998
Καββάδας Δημήτριος, *Εικονογραφημένον Βοτανικόν και Φυτολογικόν Λεξικόν,* Πήγασος, Αθήνα 1956
Μπάουμαν Ἐλμουτ, *Η Ελληνική χλωρίδα στο μύθο στην τέχνη, στη λογοτεχνία,* Ε. Ε. Προστασίας της Φύσεως, Αθήνα 1993
Φραγκάκη Ευαγγελία, *Συμβολή εις την δημώδη ορολογίαν των φυτών,* Αθήνα 1969
Φραγκάκη Ευαγγελία, *Η δημώδης ιατρική της Κρήτης,* Αθήνα 1978
Χελντράϊχ Θεόδωρος, *Λεξικό των δημωδών ονομάτων των φυτών της Ελλάδος,* Αφοι Τολίδη, Αθήνα 1980